Massimo Modonesi, Alfonso García Vela and
María Vignau Loría (eds.)

The Concept of Social Class in
Contemporary Marxist Theory

Massimo Modonesi, Alfonso García Vela and
María Vignau Loría (eds.)

THE CONCEPT OF SOCIAL CLASS IN CONTEMPORARY MARXIST THEORY

Bibliografische Information der Deutschen Nationalbibliothek
Die Deutsche Nationalbibliothek verzeichnet diese Publikation in der Deutschen Nationalbibliografie; detaillierte bibliografische Daten sind im Internet über http://dnb.d-nb.de abrufbar.

Bibliographic information published by the Deutsche Nationalbibliothek
Die Deutsche Nationalbibliothek lists this publication in the Deutsche Nationalbibliografie; detailed bibliographic data are available in the Internet at http://dnb.d-nb.de.

Cover image: *Il Quarto Stato*, Giuseppe Pellizza da Volpedo (1901). Public Domain.

ISBN-13: 978-3-8382-1607-2
© *ibidem*-Verlag, Stuttgart 2022
Alle Rechte vorbehalten

Das Werk einschließlich aller seiner Teile ist urheberrechtlich geschützt. Jede Verwertung außerhalb der engen Grenzen des Urheberrechtsgesetzes ist ohne Zustimmung des Verlages unzulässig und strafbar. Dies gilt insbesondere für Vervielfältigungen, Übersetzungen, Mikroverfilmungen und elektronische Speicherformen sowie die Einspeicherung und Verarbeitung in elektronischen Systemen.

All rights reserved. No part of this publication may be reproduced, stored in or introduced into a retrieval system, or transmitted, in any form, or by any means (electronic, mechanical, photocopying, recording or otherwise) without the prior written permission of the publisher. Any person who does any unauthorized act in relation to this publication may be liable to criminal prosecution and civil claims for damages.

Printed in the EU

Table of Contents

Introduction
Massimo Modonesi 7

Chapter 1
From Marx to Lenin: class and class struggle
Alfonso García Vela 13

Chapter 2
Gramsci and the subaltern classes
Guido Liguori 37

Chapter 3
Thompson and the experience of class
María Vignau Loría 53

Chapter 4
Poulantzas and the structuration of classes
María Vignau Loría 69

Chapter 5
Wright and class in Analytical Marxism
María Vignau Loría 93

Chapter 6
From mass-worker to multitude: the metamorphosis of the class subject in Italian *operaismo* and post-*operaismo*
Massimo Modonesi and Matari Pierre Manigat 117

Chapter 7
Open Marxism and class as struggle
Alfonso García Vela 133

Chapter 8
Final reflections: on the sociological relevance of the Marxist concept of social class
Massimo Modonesi 155

Notes on Contributors 165

Introduction

Massimo Modonesi

Marx was too modest about his contribution to the study of social classes and their struggle when he said, in his enthusiasm for conceptual precision, that he had not found the "existence of classes in modern society nor the struggle between them". Indeed, his perspective of class struggle and classes in struggle turned out to be a theoretical revolution that established a new principle for the understanding of the dynamics of modern societies, as well as their historical evolution more generally. At the same time, it was ironically prophetic in relation to his own work agenda, given that his production was interrupted precisely when he arrived at the anatomy and definition of social classes. Marx was not able to display all the implications of his findings on social classes with respect to capital. However, he did establish a set of coordinates that allow us to think about them.

These coordinates led to the development of one of the most fecund, creative and debated areas within Marxism, with Marx and beyond Marx: an area that looked for elements to characterize and understand classes and their struggle in the intersection between theoretical abstraction and the concrete sociohistorical transformations of capitalism.

These reflections on the concept of social class need to be recovered and emphasized in order to evaluate their importance and scope within Marxist sociological theory. Additionally, in order to face the challenge of understanding and explaining contemporary capitalist societies, there is a need to elucidate the ground in which it is possible to have a contemporary theoretical debate on the relevance of social classes and their struggle. In this way, this collective book presents necessary conceptual clarifications for new and future attempts to think about a central category of the Marxist critique to contemporary social reality.

In the chapters of this book, we present a series of contributions to the Marxist definition of the concept of *social class* through the voice of a series of authors, as well as the connections between them. In other words, we present explicit and implicit debates.

Going from classic to contemporary authors, we consider theorists that provided contributions that became representative of trends, schools of thought and original theoretical perspectives, and that grew into the backbone of Marxist thought: Karl Marx, Vladimir Lenin, Antonio Gramsci, Edward Palmer Thompson, Nicos Poulantzas, Erik O. Wright, Antonio Negri and John Holloway, with references to Rosa Luxemburg, Georg Lukács, and Ralph Miliband.

We recognize that the treatment and the very selection of authors implies a relatively arbitrary cut. However, given the impossibility of exhaustiveness, we selected thinkers that were particularly original in their propositions and unarguably far-reaching within the Marxist debate and the history of the concept of social class, particularly in the field of social theory and sociology. We can thus say that we are not missing any contemporary author that is considered indispensable in regards to originality, salience and significance.

Additionally, for reasons of order and clarity, as well as time and space, we decided to limit ourselves to the analysis of the work of our selected authors; we trace their main arguments and ideas without including references to the interpretations and controversies that each one brought forth. Such would require both a specific treatment and an extension which exceeded by far our aim for synthesis. We think that many of our readers will be undergraduate and graduate students, so we tried to synthesize the ideas of the authors without overwhelming the text (and our readers) with our observations and comments, nor those of others that deviate the lines of argument.

While we emphasized contemporary contributions and debates, we decided to include a first chapter that reconstructs the arguments from Marx and Lenin, so that our readers understand the starting points of these classical thinkers, which have so decisively influenced the debate on the concept of social class. This first chapter discusses the conformation and configuration of classes, the constitution of bourgeois society through class struggle and, in the political field of action, the ideas around class consciousness and the struggle for the abolition of classes. All subsequent Marxists tried to develop and rethink these topics, including the tension and articulation between the economic and political dimensions of class struggle.

We use a chronological criterion to present the authors' arguments in relation to the production and circulation of their work, even when the debates branched out and developed in non-linear ways. We thus lay out a sequence of authors that left a mark on two crucial moments in the Marxist debate: that of its expansion, during the post-war and until the 70s, and that of its reaction to the crisis, from the 80s and until the present time.

The second chapter is dedicated to the Italian Marxist Antonio Gramsci, who wrote during the 20s and 30s, but whose work was only known at the end of the 40s and the beginning of the 50s. This chapter highlights his contribution to the debate with the concept of *subaltern classes*; a formulation of Marxist origin that has been particularly resistant to the passage of time and widely used in current sociological and philosophical debates, from Marxist to neo- or post-Marxist ones. Under this formulation, Gramsci tried to think of class subjectivity in regards to the relationship between command and obedience, as the subjective counterpart to the practice of hegemony. Aside from the nominal reception of the notion of *subaltern*, this conceptualization opens the way for subsequent works that think about the conformation of class subjectivities in the context of relations of domination. In other words, it opens the way to authors that acknowledge the sociopolitical and cultural aspects of capitalism without losing sight of the relations of exploitation in the background.

The third chapter is explores the work of Marxist historian E.P. Thompson, whose most important work was developed during the 60s. Thompson proposed a notion that emerged from his historiographic research and is condensed in a conceptualization that highlights the procedural and relational character of social class. It is a concept that conceives class as a historical phenomenon, grounded in the terrain of social relations rather than structures. Furthermore, it emphasizes the experience and subjectivation of the objective conditions of exploitation and domination. Thompson's conceptualization features class struggle and class consciousness as moments that exist and emerge at the same time as classes themselves—classes exist because they are in struggle.

The fourth chapter analyzes Nicos Poulantzas' concept of social class. Poulantzas was a Greek sociologist and philosopher identified with structural Marxism, whose work spans over the 60s and 70s. This chapter explores a conceptualization of social class characterized by its grounding in the most classic—and occasionally tough—elements of Marxism. Poulantzas' work developed from a theoretical background of structural determinism (economic in-the-last-instance), but it still incorporates innovation and creativity by assigning a privileged role to social practices, political contradiction, and struggle.

The fifth chapter explores the work of Erik Olin Wright, an American sociologist who was a member of the Analytical Marxism school. Wright took on the challenge of formulating a concept of social class that linked the theoretical analysis of structural processes to empirically observable phenomena, particularly in regards to "middle or indeterminate classes" as concrete elements of the contemporary class structure. Wright's work stands out for its incorporation of elements and concerns related to the empirical analysis of classes. However, it is still firmly grounded in a Marxist agenda that conceptualizes class as an antagonistic relation of exploitation and gives centrality to the notions of struggle and class consciousness.

The sixth chapter presents a summary of the contributions of Italian o*peraismo* and post-*operaismo*, particularly in reference to Antonio Negri's work, an author whose intellectual production and influence has extended well into the 21st century. His main contributions make reference to the distinct forms adopted by social labor in the different phases of contemporary capitalism, expressed in the succession of the concepts mass-worker, social worker and multitude. These three categories serve to delineate the perimeter and assign content to what has been defined as class recomposition. Furthermore, they are conceptualized as having dynamic preeminence and autonomy with respect to capital, which is constantly trying to disarrange and break down the subjective recomposition of class in its different historical expressions.

The seventh chapter is dedicated to the so-called Open Marxism and focuses on the work by Richard Gunn, Werner Bonefeld and John Holloway. This perspective considers the separation of the notions of class and struggle as the fetishization of class. Accordingly, it adopts a critical approach to the existence and definition of class; it denies the possibility of identity affirmation, and conceives the dynamics of struggle as a manifestation of the existence of an impulse towards the self-determination of anticapitalist subjectivities.

This book does not pretend to draw any conclusions regarding a choice between one proposal or another, nor does it attempt to depict an eclectic solution. Rather, it seeks to provide a solid basis for the knowledge of the main contributions in contemporary Marxism, and to place the debate on the concept of social class at the center of current sociological reflections. Along these lines, the last chapter is not a balance nor an assessment of the work of the authors analyzed in this book. Instead, it is an exercise in the problematization of the concepts of struggle and class, which aims to highlight their relevance and potential in Marxist sociology, within an agenda centered in the principle of antagonism.

We wrote this book with the aim to recognize and revitalize the Marxist perspective on the study of social class. Beyond that goal, we also hope to offer tools for reflection that will allow our readers to refresh and expand upon their knowledge on a fundamental concept and a debate of great theoretical import for the study of contemporary societies.

Chapter 1

From Marx to Lenin: class and class struggle

Alfonso García Vela

Introduction

This chapter intends to approach the issue of class and class struggle in the critical theory of Karl Marx and the theory of praxis of Lenin. Marx was a theorist of class struggle and remains a fundamental reference point for the modern theory of social classes, while Lenin's definition of class determined the idea of class in the 20th century. Lenin (1919) defines class basically as "groups of men" differentiated according to their location, relation, and role in capitalist production. In the work of Marx there is no definitive concept of class or a definition in the strict sense; sometimes it appears as constituted groups and, others, as the result of relations of struggle.

In a letter addressed to Joseph Weydemer in 1852, Marx (1978, p. 220) wrote what he considered were his contributions to class theory:

> "And now as to myself, no credit is due to me for discovering the existence of classes in modern society or the struggle between them. Long before me bourgeois historians had described the historical development of this class struggle and bourgeois economists, the economic anatomy of the classes. What I did that was new was to prove: (1) that the existence of classes is only bound up with particular historical phases in the development of production, (2) that the class struggle necessarily leads to the dictatorship of the proletariat, (3) that this dictatorship itself only constitutes the transition to the abolition of all classes and to a classless society".

In this letter, Marx acknowledges that he did not discover social classes; classic economists such as David Ricardo wrote on class before he did[1]. However, unlike classic economists, Marx considers class and class struggle to be fundamental determinations in history

---

[1] On the issue of classes in Ricardo and Marx, see Heinrich (2004).

and its development. Despite his great contributions to the understanding of class and class struggle, Marx did not develop a class theory in systematic terms; consequently, it is very difficult to precisely describe his concept of class. Furthermore, his theoretical reflections on class run through the entirety of his work.

As a result, great Marxist theorists set out to develop a theory of class based on their own understanding of Marx's critical theory. Lenin, one of the most important Marxist politicians and theorists of the past century, interpreted the work of Marx on the basis of the great historical changes of the 20th century and developed his own revolutionary theory and practice, prevailing over other Marxist currents and interpretations. The center of Lenin's theorizing is revolutionary political practice. As we shall see further on, the concept of class is a fundamental part of his theory of praxis.

We will approach the subject of social class in Marx's theory through two books that are considered pivotal in his work: firstly, the Manifesto of the Communist Party, which he co-authored with Engels. In this text, class and class struggle are at the center of history up to present. Although the issue of class and class struggle is very present in other works by Marx, such as The Class Struggles in France, the Eighteenth Brumaire of Luis Bonaparte or The German Ideology, in Communist Manifesto it is at the very core of the argumentation (Heinrich, 2004). In this sense, Manifesto is the work of Marx that implicitly includes a class theory which is, at the same time, a theory of the abolition of classes. Therefore, we believe it is greatly relevant in understanding the notion of class in Marx's theorizing. It must be underlined that, for Marx, the idea of class was also a means of political upheaval. A concept that was linked to the proletariat and drove it to political action, to revolutionary struggle.[2]

Furthermore, in Manifesto Marx and Engels develop the relation between class and struggle, an idea that is fundamental for E.P. Thompson and Open Marxism. In Manifesto, the notion of class is

---

[2] According to Th. W. Adorno (2003, p. 94) "the concept of class is bound up with the emergence of the proletariat and class theory was a means of political upheaval".

intertwined with politics: for Marx and Engels (2012, p. 46) "every class struggle is a political struggle". In struggle, proletarians have nothing to lose but their chains, but they can win the entire world. According to the preface to the 1882 Russian edition, Marx and Engels set out to proclaim "the inevitable impending dissolution of modern bourgeois property". In other words, in Manifesto the proletarian class is called upon to overturn all existing social order, and theory aims at providing proletarians certainty in victory. Moreover, in this book the communist party appears as the organization where the working class finally finds its realization and revolutionary mission, an idea that Lenin will take up in his classic work What is to Be Done? In many aspects, one could say that Communist Manifesto is a precursor to Lenin's theory of praxis.

The second book by Marx that we will touch upon in this chapter is Capital, more specifically the last chapter of Volume III, titled Classes. We consider the last chapter of Volume III to be relevant in the study of class in Marx's theorizing. Its relevance lies in that, on the one hand, it is the last work by Marx on social classes and, on the other, although there is a 20-year interval between Manifesto and Capital, our author seems to uphold the same theoretical perspective on class and the relation between class and struggle that he deployed in his earlier works.

As in the work of Marx, the concept of class also permeates the work of Lenin. His reflections on class consciousness, organization, the party, the dictatorship of the proletariat, and socialism imply a notion of class. In this chapter, we will approach the concept of class in Lenin's theory through his most famous work: *What is to Be Done?* published in 1902. In this book, Lenin uses the problem of how to achieve class consciousness amongst workers as a starting point to unfold his theory of revolutionary organization. Finally, as we have already mentioned, in the work of Lenin — unlike that of Marx — one does find a conceptual definition of class. As we shall see, this definition appears in a text that was published in the form of a pamphlet during the first years of the Russian Revolution, titled *A Great Beginning*. Soviet economists such as David I. Rosenberg (1979) have gone as far as to claim that Lenin's definition of social class appearing in *A Great Beginning* originates directly from Marx's chapter on classes in *Volume III* of *Capital*.

History and class struggle

The Communist Manifesto is amongst the most important political works of Marx and Engels; according to Eric Hobsbawm (2012, p. 4), it is the most influential political work since the Declaration of the Rights of the Man and of the Citizen. It was first published in London in 1848, a few days before the revolution that began in Paris and spread across central Europe. The revolution in which the organized workers movement showed its might to the capitalist class for the first time. Arguably, this event foretold a new era in class struggle, one in which communist parties would play a crucial role, and Manifesto presented the theory and practice of communists in class struggle. Manifesto was written by Marx and Engels at the request of the Communist League, an international workers association previously named the League of the Just. Marx and Engels joined in 1847 and, on that same year, the League was reorganized and renamed as Communist Leagues, influenced by Marx and Engel's "critical communism" (Hobsbawm, 2012, p. 3).

In the *Preface* to the German edition of 1872, Marx and Engels (1978, p. 469) mention that, during the party *Congress* held in London in 1847, they were entrusted with composing a theoretical and practical program for the party that was to be published. It was to be theoretical, in the sense of the analysis of bourgeois society as a whole, and practical in exposing the tactics of the communists, which varied depending on the situation and historical circumstances of each country. Since its publication, it has been translated into many languages and printed in many countries around the world. In this same *Preface,* our authors claim that, although their conditions changed in the 25 years that had gone by since its publication and *Manifesto* had become a historical document, the fundamental principles contained therein are still correct today. Following Marx's death, in the prefaces that were published in the subsequent editions of *Manifesto*, Engels attributed these principles solely and exclusively to Marx; therefore, when referring to them we will only reference Marx.

From the first chapter of *Manifesto*, Marx (2012, p. 34-35) argues that "the history of all hitherto existing society is the history of class struggles". Before examining classes throughout history, Marx posits class struggle. The starting point of his analysis is the struggle between the oppressors and the oppressed. According to Marx's critical theory, class struggle is a permanent feature in history, at times concealed and at times open. Furthermore, history itself is driven by confrontation, by the antagonism between the oppressors and the oppressed. In different eras, class antagonisms have assumed diverse forms; however, no matter what form they assumed, "one fact is common to all past ages, viz., the exploitation of one part of society by the other" (Marx & Engels, 2012, p. 59).

This assertion is a critique against all history of humanity, a critique against the exploitation and injustice that have existed throughout history and which persist in different forms in present-day capitalism. However, for our authors the history of humanity is not a history of domination; on the contrary, it is a history of struggle, a struggle that becomes the driving force of historical change that gives birth to classes. Class struggle concludes in the revolutionary transformation of all society and in the collapse of classes. Bourgeois society was born out of class struggle, it continues to develop within and through it, and it will be terminated by class struggle.

The bourgeois class

In the first chapter, Marx and Engels present the classes and class divisions of the old societies and of the modern bourgeois society. In Rome there were patricians, knights, plebeians, and slaves and in the Middle Ages there were feudal lords, vassals, tradesmen, and servants. The bourgeois society emerged from the class struggle that culminated in the collapse of feudal society; a central characteristic of bourgeois society is that it simplified class contradictions. In this society we find two enemy camps, two big classes that directly oppose each other: the bourgeoisie or capitalist class, the modern owners of the means of production; and the proletarians or working class, those expropriated from the means of production who, for this reason, are forced to sell their labor power in order to subsist. Marx and Engels point out that bourgeois society has not abolished classes or their contradictions, but simply replaced old classes, previous conditions of exploitation and past forms of struggle with new ones.

Furthermore, Marx and Engels describe how class struggle has shaped and transformed the bourgeois class and the working class. The bourgeois class is the result of great political struggles and of a series of transformations in the mode of production and exchange. The bourgeoisie was created on the basis of classes that were oppressed during the rule of feudal lords; the struggles of the bourgeois class gradually transformed their conditions of existence and put an end to the old mode of feudal exploitation. The mode of feudal exploitation collapsed when it ceased to satisfy the demand of the new markets; manufacture emerged, but it was met with the same fate: collapse, caused by the constant growth of the markets.

Manufacture was replaced by the great modern industry, and with it appeared the modern bourgeois and a new form of exploitation: surplus value, a concept coined by Marx many years later, in *Capital*. The modern bourgeois or millionaire industrialists turned into "leaders of the whole industrial armies" (Marx & Engels, 2012, p. 36). The economic success of the bourgeoisie occurred in parallel with political success, propelling it to the conquest of power and, therefore, to class rule.

It must be stressed that Manifesto contains an instrumental idea of the state, one which greatly influenced the state theories that prevailed in the left until the 1960s, such as the theory of state monopoly capitalism and the theory of the state in social democracy.[3] In Manifesto, Marx and Engels (2012, p. 37) point out that "the executive of the modern state is but a committee for managing the common affairs of the whole bourgeoisie". Here the state appears as an instrument of the bourgeoisie for the safeguarding of its class interests. However, when the communist revolution triumphs, the proletariat will use state power to expropriate the means of

---

[3] On the theory of state monopoly capitalism and the theory of the state in social democracy, see Clarke (1991).

production from the bourgeoisie and concentrate them in the state. The latter turns into a neutral territory of class struggle of sorts, which can be seized by the proletarians and used as an indispensable means to radically transform the capitalist mode of production. In Manifesto, the state is perceived as an instrument for domination or emancipation, depending on the class that is in power.

In later years, Marx reformulated his conception of the state. In Grundrisse, the draft of Capital written ten years after Manifesto, Marx (1993, p. 108) conceives the state as "the Concentration of bourgeois society", a perspective that implies that the fundamental function of the state is to ensure the totality of capitalist social relations.[4] In this sense, the state is constituted by relations of domination; therefore, human emancipation entails its abolition. For Marx, communism involves the abolition of capitalism and its forms of existence such as the state. We can say that Marx's theory is not a theory on the state, as liberal theories are, but a critical theory of the state. In the 1872 preface of Communist Manifesto, Marx and Engels (2012, p. 78) criticize the instrumental idea of the state and write in reference to the experience of the Paris Commune: "one thing especially was proven by the Commune, viz., "that the working class cannot simply lay hold of the ready-made state machinery, and wield it for its own purposes"". However, if we assume that Manifesto contains an inadequate theorization of the state, what is relevant in this text is that it shows us that the starting point for a critical theory of the state is class struggle. Therefore, a Marxist analysis of the state involves a notion of class and class struggle.

In *Manifesto*, Marx and Engels (2012, p. 40) point out that wherever the bourgeoisie has conquered power, it has destroyed feudal relations; at the same time, it has subordinated the countryside to the city, rural populations to urban populations, the East to the West, and it has created enormous cities. The rise of the bourgeoisie "has agglomerated population, centralized the means of production, and has concentrated property in a few hands". In addition, it has managed to dominate the forces of nature, employ machines, apply science, navigate, conquer the railway, communications, and

---

[4] On the fundamental function of the state, see Hirsch (2005).

agriculture. In a nutshell, it has led to a continuous revolution in the relations of production and in all social relations. As never before in the history of humanity, the bourgeois class has developed enormous productive forces to such an extent that it has created the possibility of the material emancipation of humankind.[5]

However, it has simultaneously created social relations of production that stand in the way of this possibility. In other words, Marx and Engels (2012, p. 42) claim that "the conditions of bourgeois society are too narrow to comprise the wealth created by them". This leads to a contradiction between the progress of the industry (productive forces) and bourgeois social relations, a contradiction that causes periodic crises in capitalist society. Here, Marx formulates the central argument of one of the most important contradictions of capitalist society: the one between the productive forces and the relations of production. In later works, such as *Contribution to the Critique of Political Economy*, *Grundrisse* or *Capital*, Marx approaches this contradiction in more detail and includes science and general social knowledge in the productive forces.

For Marx and Engels (2012, p. 41) the modern history of industry and commerce "is but the history of the revolt of modern productive forces against modern conditions of production, against the property relations that are the conditions for the existence of the bourgeoisie and of its rule". From this perspective, the overcoming of capitalism entails the abolition of bourgeois social relations, which involves the transformation of productive forces and, therefore, the suppression of the contradiction between them.

The bourgeois class seeks to overcome the crisis by destroying a mass of productive forces, intensifying the exploitation of the markets that are under its control, and conquering new markets. The bourgeoisie permanently tries to establish an equilibrium between the productive forces and the relations of production, on which its survival as a class depends; in other words, the bourgeoisie struggles for its existence as a class. According to Marx and Engels (2012, p. 46-47) "the bourgeoisie finds itself involved in a constant battle.

---

[5] On the productive forces and the material emancipation of society, see Riazanov (1974).

At first with the aristocracy; later on, with those portions of the bourgeoisie itself, whose interests have become antagonistic to the progress of industry; at all times with the bourgeoisie of foreign countries". And during its struggle and expansion, the bourgeois class shapes the world according to its own image; that is, forcing all nations and persons, if they do not want to succumb, to adopt a bourgeois existence.

The proletarian class

The bourgeoisie has not only produced powerful productive forces; at the same time, it has produced proletarians. The latter, according to Marx and Engels, are the men and women that will rise in arms and kill the bourgeois class. As in the case of the bourgeois class, the emergence of the proletarian class is closely linked to its struggles; Marx and Engels (2012, p. 44) write that "the proletariat goes through various stages of development. With its birth begins its struggle with the bourgeoisie". The struggle commences with isolated workers and continues with the workers of an entire factory; subsequently, it spreads to the workers sharing the same occupation in one area. During this period, the workers are not content with struggling only against the relations of production created by the bourgeoisie; they also struggle against the instruments of production, they break machinery and set fire to factories.

Marx and Engels (2012) point out that, at this stage, the workers are not yet united, they form a mass that is disseminated and dispersed by competition. Likewise, the are not yet combatting their true enemies but the enemies of the bourgeois class: the absolute monarchy, the non-industrial bourgeois, the petit-bourgeois and landowners. In this historical stage of working-class struggle, each victory of the workers against the enemies of the bourgeois class in in fact a victory of the bourgeoisie.

Industrial progress in the 19th century led to the increase in the number of proletarians and to their concentration in great masses in factories. Our authors point out that large masses of disorganized workers began to gain consciousness of their power and interests. In the face of their increasingly precarious situation as a result of the rise of competition between the bourgeois, commercial crises, salary fluctuations and the accelerated development of machines, workers became organized and took common action against the bourgeois; they founded associations to ensure the necessary means for their struggle.

Marx and Engels (2012, p. 45) argue that "the collisions between individual workmen and individual bourgeois take more and more the character of collisions between two classes". That is, the struggles of the proletarians, together with the progress of the industry that unites large masses of workers, transforms them from a disseminated mass of individuals into a class which threatens the continuity of bourgeois domination. Sometimes the proletarians triumph, but their victory is ephemeral. For our authors, "the real fruit of their battles lies not in the immediate result but in the ever-expanding union of the workers"; that is, the union of workers entails their constitution as class, and as a class they confront bourgeois domination in a direct and condensed way, endangering the continuity of the system.

The unity of proletarians leads to their organization in and for struggle; the proletarian class is precisely the organization of proletarians in struggle. What is more, for Marx and Engels (2012, p. 46) "every class struggle is a political struggle", therefore, the organization of the proletariat in a class involves its organization in a political party. But not any party; the proletariat must organize in a party that advocates the common interests of all the proletarian movement, regardless of the nationality of the proletarians and the different stages in which the struggle between the proletariat and the bourgeoisie might find itself. The "Party" that Marx and Engels (2012, p. 51–52) refer to is the party of the communists, the theoretical and practical vanguard of all proletarian parties and of the proletariat itself. According to our authors, the immediate goals of the communists are: "formation of the proletariat into a class, overthrow of the bourgeois supremacy, conquest of political power by the proletariat".

Class and Party: Marx, Engels and Lenin

For Marx and Engels (2012, p. 51) the communists "are, on the one hand, practically, the most advanced and resolute section of the working-class parties of every country, that section which pushes forward all others; on the other hand, theoretically, they have over the great mass of the proletariat the advantage of clearly understanding the line of march, the conditions, and the ultimate general results of the proletarian movement". We can interpret the aforementioned arguments as stating that politics maintains a certain autonomy from bourgeois social relations. That is, politics is understood as an instance that is somewhat separated and autonomous from capital, from which one can intervene in society in a revolutionary way, through institutions such as the political party or the state. This perspective allows for the establishment of a direct link between struggle, organization, class, and party. The ultimate meaning of class is its organization in the "Party"; it is at this point that we find the precursor to Lenin's theoretical reflection. Hence the claim that his most important work, *What is to Be Done?*, is in a sense a theoretical development of the political ideas included in *Communist Manifesto*.

Furthermore, *Communist Manifesto* anticipates how politics will be done in the 20th century. According to Lazarus (2007), the basis of political struggle in the 19th century was insurrection; the *Paris Commune* of 1870 is a very important example of that idea of politics. In the 20th century, however, a new mode of political struggle emerges, in which the party becomes fundamental. In the 20th century, the idea of political struggle is centered in the party, whereby the issues of class and access to power are organized. In this sense, Lenin turned the idea of doing politics in the 20th century into the condition of his revolutionary strategy. Lazarus (2007, p. 258-259) deploys a very intriguing thesis: In *What is to Be Done?* Lenin breaks with the thesis that Marx and Engels present in *Manifesto* "with regard to the spontaneous character of the appearance of communists within the modern proletariat. In contrast to the Marxist thesis that can be stated as Where there are proletarians, there are Communists".

The thesis of Lazarus points out that, for Marx, the appearance of communists is intrinsic to the existence of the proletarians as a class; in other words, the existence of a spontaneous revolutionary political consciousness in proletarians is possible, which means that their own self-emancipation is also possible. However, Lenin distances himself from Marx's thesis and argues that revolutionary consciousness in proletarians is not a spontaneous phenomenon, it is the party that brings revolutionary consciousness to the proletarians from the outside and allows them to organize for revolutionary struggle. Thus, in his theory, Lenin prefigures the way of doing politics in the 20th century. Likewise, Badiou (2007, p. 9) points out that what is real in revolutionary politics is a condition for Lenin's theory; this is a perspective that determined political subjectivity in the 20th century, whereby what is real is "what is immediately practicable, here and now".

In *What is to Be Done?* Lenin develops his theory of revolutionary organization, using the problem of how to develop class consciousness in workers as his starting point. For Lenin (2012) it is crucial to show the meaning of the spontaneous element and the conscious element in class struggle. According to Lenin (2012, p. 170) the popular movement that emerged in Russia at the end of the 19th century had a spontaneous character, that is, a "consciousness in an embryonic form"; many of the riots were simply uprisings of oppressed and angry people. In certain strikes there were sparks of consciousness such as the formulation of specific demands, the anticipation of the most convenient element, the discussion of cases and examples from other places, etc. However, the strikes were simply that, sparks of consciousness and embryonic states of class struggle.

What Lenin (2012) wanted to show was that workers could not acquire a class consciousness by themselves or spontaneously, as a result of their struggles. According to Lenin, the history of all countries shows that by way of its own means the working class can only establish a trade-unionist consciousness; that is, the conviction that they must group in trade unions, struggle against their employers, demand the promulgation of laws that are indispensable for workers, etc. Likewise, for Lenin the spontaneous movement leads to the supremacy of the bourgeois ideology. Lenin argued that it is not true that class consciousness or the consciousness of the possibility and necessity of socialism is the inevitable and direct outcome of the struggles of the proletarian class.

According to Lenin (2012, p. 187) the consciousness of the modern class "can arise only on the basis of profound scientific knowledge". A knowledge that the working class does not possess; consequently, class consciousness can only be brought to workers from the outside: by the intellectuals with profound scientific knowledge. This is one of Lenin's most important and controversial thesis. The proletarian is not the bearer of science, the intellectuals are; therefore, class consciousness is something introduced from the outside. Lenin stressed that the doctrine of socialism emerged from philosophical, historical and economic theories that have been elaborated by intellectuals. As an example of intellectuals with profound scientific, philosophical and historical knowledge he mentions Marx and Engels, the founders of modern scientific socialism. The intellectuals that created modern socialism transmitted their knowledge to proletarians who stood out by virtue of their intellectual development; and the outstanding proletarians introduced the knowledge they acquired in class struggle wherever the historical conditions allowed it. It must be added that, for Lenin, knowledge is not neutral; it is an instrument of class struggle. Theory is at the service of a class interest regardless of the intentions of the intellectuals themselves; it cannot be otherwise in a society that is permeated by class struggle (Kolakowski, 1980).

For Lenin, revolutionary intellectuals must organize in the party, and the fundamental task of the revolutionary party is to bring to the proletariat consciousness of their situation and their mission — that is, class consciousness. There would be no need to do this if class consciousness were the spontaneous outcome of the struggles of the proletariat. According to Lenin (2012, p. 192) the support of revolutionaries to the spontaneous movement must be fought against, for it leads to the supremacy of the bourgeois ideology. "For the simple reason that bourgeois ideology is far older in origin than Social-Democratic ideology; because it is more fully developed and because it possesses immeasurably more opportunities for being distributed". Therefore, it is a mistake to venerate the spontaneous movement; the more powerful the spontaneous movement of the masses, the higher the need for an elevated consciousness, for a theoretical, political and organizational effort.

Lenin's formulations in What is to Be Done? were the most important reference point for the revolution in the past century and led to numerous discussions and debates from different theoretical Marxist perspectives. For Georg Lúkacs (2012, p. 9) "Lenin is the greatest thinker to have been produced by the revolutionary working-class movement since Marx"; Lukacs was a Marxist theorist who assumed a more sophisticated and profound theoretical approach to Leninist issues such as class consciousness, the vanguard party and the proletarian as a historical subject. In a different Marxist tradition such as the Frankfurt School, where utopia plays a central role, Theodor Adorno (2011, p. 84) says in a conversation with Max Horkheimer "I have always wanted to rectify that and develop a theory that remains faithful to Marx, Engels and Lenin, while keeping up with culture at its most advanced.". Adorno considered that Lenin was more concerned than Marx about human subjectivity and had a more coherent understanding that, deep down, human beings are a product of society; however, Adorno rejected Lenin's idea of the vanguard party.

For her part, Rosa Luxemburg (1904), a brilliant Marxist and great revolutionary, criticized Lenin's theory of praxis and claimed that the ultra-centralism that Lenin defends is imbued by a "spirit of the overseer" and that his perception of revolutionary organization is too mechanic. For Rosa Luxemburg, the spontaneous element played an important role in the mass strikes in Russia, not only as an obstacle but also as a driving element of revolution. Furthermore, Luxemburg (2008, p. 148) argued against Lenin's idea of the intellectual as an educator or guide of sorts of the proletariat; for her, "revolutions do not allow anyone to play the schoolmaster with them".

We have seen that in *What is to Be Done?* the proletarian class, class interests, class consciousness and all things related to the struggle of the working class are condensed within revolutionary organization in the form of the vanguard party. In other words, in

Lenin's theorizing, the notion of class and class struggle acquires its ultimate meaning in the communist Party. This theoretical perspective can already be found in Marx and Engel's *Communist Manifesto*. For Marx, Engels, and Lenin, the party of the communists is the organized class. Therefore, the communist party is where the proletarian class finally attains its realization and its mission, which is none other than the overturning of bourgeois domination. However, it must be stressed that there is a fundamental difference between Marx and Lenin: Marx considers the self-emancipation of the working class possible, while Lenin considers that its liberation can only be achieved through the party.

According to *Manifesto*, the first step of the revolution is the taking of power and the rise of the proletariat to a dominant class. It is through revolution that the proletariat turns into the ruling class and breaks with bourgeois social relations. Finally, when the proletarian class suppresses the bourgeois relations of production, class antagonism—and, consequently, classes—will be abolished. From the abolition of the old bourgeois society and its classes "we shall have an association in which the free development of each is the condition for the free development of all" (Marx & Engels, 2012, p. 62–63). Thus, in *Manifesto*, the proletarian class fights for the abolition of its own existence as class. However, despite all our discussion on class struggle and its organization, we have still not answered the question: what is class for Lenin and Marx?

What is class? Lenin and Marx

It is easier to approach the Leninist concept of class, given that Lenin defined class in a text that was published as a pamphlet more than 15 years before *What is to Be Done?*, titled *A Great Beginning*. In this pamphlet, Lenin reflects on voluntary work and its importance for class struggle. Voluntary work was an initiative of workers and communist sympathizers that was staged on Saturdays during the first years of the Bolshevik Revolution and was called *Communist Saturdays*. For Lenin (1919, p. 18), *Communist Saturdays* were enormously important because "they demonstrate the conscious and spontaneous initiative of the workers in their endeavor to increase the productivity of labor during the transition to the new labor discipline, in the creation of Socialist conditions of life and work".

Reflecting on class struggle and the tasks of the proletariat after taking political power, Lenin (1919, p. 15) defines classes as:

> "large groups of people distinguished from one another by their status in an historically-determined system of social production, by the proportion of the means of wealth production they possess, by the part they play in the social organization of labor, and by the kind and the quantity of socially produced wealth they have at their disposal. In a class society there are groups of men who, by virtue of their favored position in the social order, can appropriate the results of the labor of other groups".

For Lenin, social classes are basically groups of humans constituted on the basis of their relation with the means of production; its relation with the means of production allows one group to appropriate the work of another group. In capitalist society, the bourgeois class owns the means of production, a condition that allows it to appropriate the surplus value created by the labor of the working class. The concept of class is, for Lenin, a starting point to explain the meaning of the "suppression of classes" which is the final goal of socialism.

Based on the concept of class, Lenin (1919) concludes that to completely suppress social classes it is not enough to overturn the exploiters and suppress their property. All private property of the means of production must be abolished, as well as the differences between the city and the countryside, between manual and intellectual labor. In the transition from capitalism to socialism, this task can only be accomplished by the strongest and more advanced class in bourgeois society, the working class.

It is considerably harder to answer the question of what class is for Marx, given that in his work there exists no final concept of class or a definition in the strict sense of the word. Therefore, on the basis of the previous discussion, we will try to approach the core or central premise of his idea of class. In Manifesto, the starting point for the concept of class is struggle. Classes are not groups that are formed before the struggle; the proletariat and the bourgeoisie are constituted as classes in the course of the historical movement of their struggle. In principle, we can say that, for Marx, class is intrinsic to struggle.⁶ The German Ideology, written by Marx and Engels with only a few years difference from Manifesto, displays the same theoretical perspective. Our authors argue that "the separate individuals form a class only insofar as they have to carry on a common battle against another class; in other respects they are on hostile terms with each other as competitors" (Marx & Engels, 1998, p. 85).

In his most important work, *Capital: A Critique of Political Economy*, published nearly twenty years after *Manifesto* and *The German Ideology*, Marx analyses how the working class was shaped through the struggles for the regulation of the working day in the different periods of capitalism. The explanation provided by Marx in the chapter titled "The Working Day" in *Volume I* of *Capital* refers precisely to the long and difficult struggle of the working class to achieve legislation on working hours. Marx (1990, p. 416) points out that "for 'protection' against 'the serpent of their agonies,' the laborers must put their heads together, and, as a class, compel the passing of a law, an all-powerful social barrier that shall prevent the very workers from selling, by voluntary contract with capital, themselves and their families into slavery and death". The isolated worker is defenseless in the face of capital; but when workers organize in the struggle as a working class, they confront the domination of the capitalist class in a direct and concentrated way.

Having said that, what else does Marx tell us about classes in *Capital*? The issue of class and class struggle is present from the very first chapters of the book. It does not appear openly, in many chapters it is veiled, it arises as an intrinsic part of the unfolding of categories. From the first chapter we are informed that there is an antagonism between value and use value within commodity, a struggle for the rule of value over use value; that capital cannot exist without value, and that labor is use value *par excellence*.⁷ Thus, the

---

⁶   On the relation between class and struggle, see Thompson (1978) and Gunn (1987).

⁷   In Grundrisse, Marx (1993, p. 295) points out that "in this relation between labor and capital, and already in this first relation of exchange between the two, that the worker here buys the exchange value and the capitalist the use value, in that labor confronts capital not as a use value, but as the use value pure and simple".

struggle between capital and labor—that is, class struggle—is already present in the commodity itself. However, as we shall see in what follows, the last chapter of *Volume III* of *Capital* is greatly relevant, for it is in this chapter that Marx specifically analyses the issue of class.

In his lifetime, Marx only published *Volume I* of *Capital*; *Volume II* and *Volume III* were published by Engels after his death based on a series of manuscripts and notes that our author left behind. In the *Preface* to *Volume III* of *Capital*, Engels writes that Marx was involved in great projects in the 1860s. Not only was he preparing books II and II of *Capital*, he was also handing in book I for printing and was very engaged in the huge endeavor of founding and setting in motion the International Workingmen's Association. Furthermore, those years were exceedingly hard for Marx and his family because of the extreme poverty they were living in.[8]

In his last years, Marx faced many health problems as a result of that painful period in his life and the excess of work; this submerged him in periods of intellectual inactivity. For that reason, Marx did not conclude his theoretical project, including class theory. Our author died in March 1883 without concluding Volume II and III of Capital. On the last chapter of Volume III that speaks of classes, Engels points out that Marx only left the first part; the mentioned chapter is a final synthesis of sorts, and Marx used to leave synthesis for the last stage of the composition, before handing his work over for printing.

Marx (1981) begins the chapter on classes by presenting the three great classes of modern society founded on the capitalist regime of production: firstly, the workers, who own their labor power

---

[8] On that extremely difficult period for Marx and his family, see Dussel (1988, p. 15): "On 25 February 1862, Marx wrote to Engels telling that 'taking all in all, leading such a dog's life is hardly worthwhile'. And on 18 June, he communicated again to his friend: 'Every day my wife says she wishes she and the children were safely in their graves, and I really cannot blame her, for the humiliations, torments and alarums that one has to go through in such a situation are indeed indescribable'. In September of that year, the desperate Marx considered abandoning his studies in order to devote himself to feeding his family. For this purpose, he intended to work as an employee on London's railway. But he failed the admission exam because of his bad handwriting."

and their income comes from their salary. Secondly, capitalists, who own capital and their source of income is profit; and, thirdly, the landowners whose source of income is the rent of the land. Marx begins the chapter with three great human groups that are differentiated on the basis of their relation to the means of production and of their source of income. In principle, we can assume that the previous idea is a definition of class that is similar to that of Lenin; but let us continue reading the chapter.

Marx points out that the most developed capitalist society can be found in England; however, in the most developed capitalism of its time one cannot observe this division into three large social classes in all its purity. In English society there are intermediate and transitionary stages that blur the dividing lines between the main social classes. Hence, one could presume the existence of strata or intermediate groups that do not correspond to the three large classes in capitalism. Nevertheless, Marx (1894) points out that the abovementioned is irrelevant for his study, given that:

> "a continual tendency and law of development of the capitalist mode of production is more and more to divorce the means of production from labor, and more and more to concentrate the scattered means of production into large groups, thereby transforming labor into wage-labor and the means of production into capital. And to this tendency, on the other hand, corresponds the independent separation of landed property from capital and labor, or the transformation of all landed property into the form of landed property corresponding to the capitalist mode of production".

Marx argues that capitalist society has the increasing tendency to split into three large social classes: the workers, the capitalists, and the landowners. That is basically the same theoretical perspective that can be found in *Manifesto*, where he posits the existence of a tendency in bourgeois society to divide society into a limited number of fundamental classes that oppose each other. However, it must be pointed out that the fundamental confrontation is the one between workers and capitalists. The landowners are, ultimately, part of the bourgeoisie.

At this point of the chapter, Marx (1981, p. 1025) writes "the question to be answered next is: What makes a class?" Why would Marx ask this question if, from the first paragraphs of this chapter, one can deduce that class is a group of humans that is differentiated from others on the basis of its relation to the means of production and its source of income? Marx (1981, p. 1026) immediately writes "this arises automatically from answering another question: 'What makes wage-laborers, capitalists and landowners the formative elements of the three great social classes?'"

Marx answers that "at first sight" the answer is the identity and source of their income. That is, what renders an individual a member of the working class is the fact that his/her income comes from a salary and that this is more or less similar to other members of the working class. The same idea can be applied to place other individuals within the capitalist class and the class of landowners, considering that capitalists make their living off profit and landowners off renting the land. According to Marx (1981, p. 1026), this standpoint is problematic for it would also imply that:

> "doctors and government officials would also form two classes, as they belong to two distinct social groups, the revenue of each group's members flowing from its own source. The same would hold true for the infinite fragmentation of interests and positions into which the division of social labor splits not only workers but also capitalists and land- owners - the latter, for instance, into vineyard-owners, field- owners, forest-owners, mine-owners, fishery-owners, etc."

Regrettably, the final chapter of Volume III of Capital is interrupted in this last paragraph. But what did Marx mean by saying that the answer to the question of what class is cannot originate from the idea that groups are determined on the basis of the identity of their income and source of income, for that would mean that professions and other economic activities can constitute a class? Marx tries to unveil what hides behind appearances, he attempts to reveal their internal link; that is why, before unmasking what hides behind the fetishized appearances of society in Capital, he often writes expressions such as "at first sight" or "appears first of all".

For example, in *Volume I* he writes "Exchange-value appears first of all as the quantitative relation, the proportion, in which use-values of one kind exchange for use-values of another kind", "A commodity appears at first sight an extremely obvious, trivial thing", etc. (Marx, 1990, pp. 126–163). Marx immediately shows us that exchange value expresses social work and that commodities are not simple objects; commodity is a type of social relation in capitalism that is manifested in an objectivized form.

These sentences are particularly interesting for they drive theoretical reflection beyond appearances, towards the content that is concealed by its forms of manifestation. In this sense, social classes "at first sight" present themselves as groups that are formed on the basis of their source of income. However, we have seen that in Manifesto and in The German Ideology the starting point for the concept of class is struggle; classes are constituted as classes in the movement of their struggle. Class struggle is the content concealed behind the forms of manifestation in capitalist society.

Consequently, we can say that Marx tried to explain the existence of class on the basis of struggle. The goal of this perspective is not only theoretical but also political. Marx's discussion on the concept of class implies answering the question on the possibility of abolishing class itself and putting an end to class society; this is one of the central issues of *Communist Manifesto* and *Capital* and one of the fundamental tasks of the working class.

The understanding of class on the basis of struggle—that is, the embracing of social relations of struggle as the starting point— does not mean class structure in capitalist society cannot be analyzed empirically, considering its relation to the means of production and the source of income of those belonging to the class. We believe it is important that theoretical reflection and class analysis be founded on the idea of struggle, for this perspective focuses on social antagonism. In other words, class is a concept that implies antagonism, conflict in capitalist social relations. In this sense, E.P. Thompson (1978, p. 149) makes an important statement when he explains that "classes do not exist as separate entities, they look around, find an enemy class and then start to struggle" On the contrary, for Thompson, as for Marx, people experience exploitation, they find points of interest and begin to fight; in this process of struggle, they discover themselves as class.

In conclusion, in Marx's critical theory class is not a category that can be found as an individual definition or can be extracted as an isolated concept, that is, outside his analysis of bourgeois social relations. That is why we cannot clearly and safely describe, in a traditional sense, the concept or definition of class in Marx's theory as we can for Lenin's concept of class. For Marx, the concept of class is an intrinsic and inseparable part of a theoretical unfolding that describes the historical movement of class struggle. In other words, the concept is part of the movement of the object itself, it is the dialectic mode of developing fundamental concepts. The very complexity of this theoretical perspective is in a sense what has allowed for the different interpretations of the concept of class.

Translated by Anna-Maeve Holloway

References

Adorno, T. W. (2003). Reflections on Class Theory. In R. Tiedemann (Ed.), *Can One Live After Auschwitz? A Philosophical Reader* (pp. 93–110). Stanford University Press.

Adorno, T. W. & Horkheimer, M. (2011). *Towards a New Manifesto*. Verso.

Badiou, A. (2007). "One Divides Itself into Two". In S. Budgen, S. Kouvelakis, & S. Zizek (Eds.), *Lenin reloaded: Toward a Politics of Truth*. Duke University Press Books.

Clarke, S. (1991). The State Debate. In Simon Clarke (Ed.), *The State Debate* (pp. 1–69). Macmillan.

Dussel, E. (2014). *Towards and Unknown Marx. A commentary on the Manuscripts of 1861–63*. Routledge.

Gunn, R. (1987). Notes on Class. *Common Sense*, 2, 15–26

Heinrich, M. (2004). *An Introduction to the three volumes of Karl Marx's Capital*. Monthly Review Press

Hirsch, J. (2005). ¿Qué significa Estado? Reflexiones acerca de la teoría del Estado capitalista. *Revista de Sociologia e Politica*, 24, 165–175.

Hobsbawm, E. (2012). Introduction. In Marx, K. & Engels, F. *The Communist Manifesto: A Modern Edition* (pp. 3–30). Verso (Kindle Edition).

Kolakowski, L. (2008) *Main Currents of Marxism: The Founders - The Golden Age - The Breakdown*. W.W. Norton & Company.

Lazarus, Sylvain. (2007). Lenin and the Party, 1902-November 1917. In S. Budgen, S. Kouvelakis, & S. Zizek (Eds.), *Lenin reloaded: Toward a Politics of Truth* (pp. 255–268). Duke University Press Books.

Lenin, V. I. (1919). *The great initiative: including the story of "Communist Saturdays"*. University of California Libraries.

Lenin, V. I. (2012). *Essential Works of Lenin: "What Is to Be Done?" and Other Writings*. Dover Publications.

Lukács, G. (2009). *Lenin: A Study on the Unity of His Thought*. Verso.

Luxemburg, R. (1904). *Organizational Questions of the Russian Social Democracy*. Available at https://www.marxists.org/archive/luxemburg/1904/questions-rsd/ch01.htm (accessed 20-05-2021)

Luxemburg, R. (2008). *The Essential Rosa Luxemburg: Reform or Revolution and the Mass Strike*. Haymarket Books.

Marx, K. (1981). *Capital: A Critique of Political Economy (Vol. 3)*. Penguin Books.

Marx, K. (1990). *Capital: A Critique of Political Economy (Vol. 1)*. Penguin Books.

Marx, K. (1993) *Grundrisse: Foundations of the Critique of Political Economy*. Penguin Books.

Marx, K., & Engels, F. (1978). *The Marx-Engels Reader*. Norton & Company

Marx, K., & Engels, F. (1998). *The German Ideology: Including Theses on Feuerbach and Introduction to The Critique of Political Economy*. Prometheus Books

Marx, Karl, & Engels, F. (2012). *The Communist Manifesto: A Modern Edition*: Verso.

Riazanov, D. (1974). *Karl Marx and Friedrich Engels*. Monthly Review Press.

Rosenberg, D. I. (1979). *Comentarios a los tres tomos de El Capital (Vol. 3)*. Editorial Ciencias Sociales.

Thompson, E. P. (1978). Eighteenth-Century English Society: Class Struggle without Class?. *Social History*, 3(2), 133–165.

Chapter 2

Gramsci and the subaltern classes[1]

Guido Liguori

In 2011 I published a study on the concept of "subaltern" in the *Prison Notebooks* and the *Letters from Prison*[2] (Liguori, 2011a). I feel the need to go back to these arguments because newer studies, with greater depth, have led me to more rigorous determinations that, while confirming the main interpretative outlines put forth in that earlier text, clarify and even correct some of the observations I made then. In particular, in this essay I will explore some Gramscian texts (from the *Notebooks* and the *Letters*) that I did not consider before, which I now believe are important in order to analyze the aforementioned concept.

In my 2011 essay I made some arguments on the considerable diffusion of the Gramscian concept of subaltern, the reasons for this diffusion, and the risks of misinterpretation observed in that literature. I will not go back to those arguments here. Instead, I will focus on the presence of that concept, and others related to it ("subaltern classes", "subaltern social groups"), in Gramsci's prison texts[3]. Indeed, it is true that the concept of "subaltern" comes up in some of the earlier writings of the Sardinian communist, even it if is not mentioned often. However, compared to the texts written in prison (which were destined to become famous), the concept had a completely different meaning — and surely a less relevant one — in the writings from the 1910s and 1920s. In the pre-prison writings, the

---

[1] This article was previously published with the title "Clases subalternas marginales y fundamentales en Gramsci" (Liguori, 2016).
[2] For reference to these arguments see Liguori (2011a). This text was also published in Spanish (Liguori, 2013).
[3] In this essay, I will make references to my 2011 text and summarize some of the arguments and observations I made there. I will make particular mention of the Gramscian texts that I did not consider then. The two essays complement each other.

concept of subaltern (inherited from the military language) indicates the intermediate degrees of the command chain, understood as a social and state-bureaucratic, military or partisan relationship. I will illustrate this with one example out of many other possible ones: in *Il paese di Pulcinella*, published in the Piedmontese edition of *Avanti!* on January 30th 1919[4], Gramsci refers to the subalterns as those who, in a well-structured bourgeois State, would be the "servants of the executive power" who comply with the orders of the high command. Alternatively, they are described as those who, in the dominant chaos, would guard their small privileges. From a social perspective, Gramsci is thinking about the "petty bourgeoisie", not about the base of the social pyramid (as he will in the *Notebooks*). In other words, he is thinking about those who occupy a middle ground in the leadership structure—both in the structure of the State and the Socialist Party[5]–, a "connecting officer" so to speak, between the high state of the bourgeoisie and the proletarian army or the mass of foot soldiers, understood as citizens and members of the proletarian mass, respectively.

The first notebooks

The word "subalterns" was already present in *Notebook 1* and it initially expressed a parallelism between social and military functions (Q1, 43, p. 133)[6]. In other words, it had the same meaning that I highlighted in the pre-prison texts. However, little by little, we see the emergence of a negative use of the concept in *Notebook 1*[7]. This new use of the concept acquires a more complex character with a meaning that could be considered as the opposite of a positive idea

---

[4] Gramsci (1984).

[5] Compare these conceptualizations with those in Gramsci (1966) and Gramsci (1971).

[6] [Translator's note (t/n): References from the *Prison Notebooks* will be cited as follows: notebook, paragraph and page. All of these quotations come from the English volumes translated and edited by J. Buttigieg (Gramsci, 2011) of the critical edition of the *Quaderni del carcere* published in Italian in 1975 and edited by Valentino Gerratana].

[7] For instance Nitti's "cunning" is defined as a "subaltern quality" (Q1, 116, p. 202) [t/n: in the English version of the *Notebooks* edited and translated by J. Buttigieg this text is found as "subordinate quality"].

of hegemonic (even if this term is not present at the moment). The Church — writes Gramsci in the note *Catholic Action* — is a "subaltern force" because it lost its own position of predominance and initiative in modernity, and is forced to being "on the defensive" (Q1, 139, p. 224). Starting in *Notebook 3*, we likewise see that the subaltern classes are those that endure the initiative of the adversaries and are being forced into a defensive position.

The first note that contains a relevant presence of the concept of subaltern is found in *Q3, 14*, "*History of the dominant class and history of the subaltern classes*". Gramsci would later retrieve it and include it as a second note in *Notebook 25* with some modifications and with a title that embellishes it: *Methodological Criteria*. This 1934 notebook compiles, as we will see, some notes on the subject of the subaltern.

Before examining the note in *Q3, 14*, it is necessary to mention that Gramsci had dedicated a prior note, *Q3, 12* to Davide (or David) Lazzaretti. The term "subaltern" does not come up here, but this note will be retrieved as the opening one for the *Notebook 25*; the "special (monothematic) one" dedicated to "the history of subaltern social groups". The reflection on Lazzaretti is then a critical element of the Gramscian reflection on the subaltern classes. Who was Davide Lazzaretti? He was a 19th century rebel, born in 1834, who founded a popular religious and heretic sect with a dense ideology of prophetic elements, in Monte Amiata, Toscana[8]. He announced his support for the Paris Commune and wanted establish a republic. The popular support he received alarmed both the Italian State and the Catholic Church. He was killed by the Italian royal army in 1878, even when he did not pose a real danger to the institutions of that time[9].

Let's now analyze the previously mentioned note in *Q3, 14*, which Gramsci will later use in the beginning of *Notebook 25*. The text is as follows:

---

[8] See Hobsbawm (1971) for more references on Lazzaretti.
[9] I analyzed this *Q13, 12* note, as well as its transcription, in the 2011 essay (p. 35 and 36).

"*History of the dominant class and history of the subaltern classes.* The history of the subaltern classes is necessarily fragmented and episodic (...) Subaltern classes are subject to the initiatives of dominant class, even when they rebel, they are in a state of anxious defense. Every trace of autonomous initiative is therefore of inestimable value. In any case, the monograph is the most suitable form of this history, which requires a very large accumulation of fragmentary material (Q3, 14, p. 23)."

What does this note tell us, even when limited to the portion transcribed above?

- First, we observe that Gramsci's words refer specifically to the *historiography* of the subaltern classes. Making history *comprehensively* and, particularly, taking into account the situation of the subaltern masses was important to the author of the *Notebooks,* since Gramsci thought that the "recognition of the national terrain" and, in this way, the knowledge of the history of the subaltern classes, was crucial[10].
- The title of this note is the very first time that the expression "subaltern classes" comes up in the *Notebooks;* in other words, this is the first time that the adjective "subaltern" refers to the term "classes". Additionally, this happened while being confronted with the expression "dominant class". Gramsci forged the concept "subaltern classes" in direct opposition to the notion of "dominant class". Thus, the new use of "subaltern" is dialectically linked to that of "dominant".
- What are the characteristics of the "subaltern classes" that Gramsci talks about? Firstly, the "dominant class" (in singular) is just one, whereas the "subaltern classes" are more than one; "subaltern classes" implies an ensemble of various social classes and fringes. This is a characteristic that must be highlighted and one upon which I will return later. Furthermore, the subaltern classes are subject to the initiatives of the dominant class but try to defend themselves; they offer hints of "autonomous initiative", which are considered valuable by Gramsci. Additionally, they are

---

[10] Compare, for instance, with Liguori, 2011 (p. 37-38).

valuable because this autonomy is the first step—only the first step—in which a different hegemony might emerge in determined conditions. The autonomy of the subaltern classes could thus be the passage from subalternity to hegemony. However, other conditions need to be also present for this transition to take place[11].
- What does Gramsci understand by "subaltern classes" in this note? We don't yet have a lot of elements to answer this question. However, based on the fact that these classes have moments of "autonomous initiative", we could say that they seem to be classes that can, at least potentially, play a certain role in the society in which they exist. In any case, I think it is important to highlight that in this note such "subaltern classes" are not placed, neither mostly nor exclusively, at the margins of history and society.

After this note, "*History of the subaltern classes*" becomes the "title" of many of Gramsci's notes in Notebook 3. That is also the case for the miscellaneous notebooks, where he uses this title to aid in the search and eventual transcription of the notes in the "special" or monothematic notebooks. For instance, "*History of the subaltern classes*" is the title of Q3, 18[12], where he talks about the "problems of Roman history", of the plebians and slaves. We see that Gramsci also uses the category of "subaltern class(es)" to talk about historical times long gone. This leads to the argument that this category is more relational than defining:

> "In the ancient and medieval State, both territorial and social (the one is but the function of the other) centralization were minimal. In a certain sense the State was a "federation" of classes: the subaltern classes had a separate life, their own institutions, etc., and sometimes these institutions had State functions (thus the phenomenon of "two governments" became extremely conspicuous during times of crisis)" (Q3, 18, p. 24).

Thus, there are situations in which the "subaltern classes" have some degree of autonomy, or even a significant one, having thus the

---

[11] The relationship between subalternity and autonomy has been investigated by Modonesi (2014), although from a different perspective.
[12] This is a text that will be claimed later in Q25, 4. I did not take these notes into account in my previous essay.

ability to produce institutions with State functions. Gramsci states that:

> "The only class excluded from having a life of its own was that of the slaves in the classical world and that of the proletarians in the medieval world. Nevertheless, even though in many respects the slaves in the antiquity and medieval proletarians found themselves in similar conditions, the situations were not identical: the uprising of the Ciompi certainly did not evoke the same sensation that a similar uprising of the slaves in Rome (Spartacus, who demands governmental power with the patricians, etc.) Whereas in the Middle Age it was possible to have an alliance between the proletariat and the people and, even more, proletarian support for the dictatorship of a prince, there was nothing of the sort in the classical world. The modern state abolishes many autonomies of the subaltern classes—it abolishes the state as a federation of classes—but certain forms of the internal life of the subaltern classes are reborn as parties, trade unions, cultural associations. The modern dictatorship abolishes those forms of class autonomy as well, and it tries hard to incorporate them into the activity of the state: in other words, the centralization of the whole life of the nation in the hands of the ruling class becomes frenetic and all-consuming." (Q3, 18, p. 24–25).

Therefore, plebians, slaves and the medieval proto-proletariat were all "subaltern classes". As mentioned in the note, they rebelled (like Spartacus) and did politics (like the uprising of the Ciompi).

In the following note in *Q3, 48*[13], Gramsci recalls the experience of the *Ordine Nuovo*. There is an interesting claim that supports our argument:

> "the element of spontaneity is therefore characteristic of the "history of the subaltern classes" and, especially, of the more marginal and peripherical elements of those classes, who have not attained a consciousness of the class per se" (Q3, 48, p. 49).

As we see, Gramsci explicitly claims here that the subaltern classes are properly differentiated from within. This category includes, as we have seen, "fundamental classes" (such as plebians and slaves, according to Marxists). However, Gramsci calls our attention to the "more marginal and peripherical elements of those classes", characterized by "spontaneity" rather than "class consciousness". He further adds in the same note:

---

[13] I only cited this text in my previous essay, but did not analyze it.

> "This unity of "spontaneity" and "conscious leadership" or "discipline" is precisely the real political action of the subaltern classes, insofar as it is mass politics and not a mere adventure by groups that appeal to the masses" (Q3, 48, p. 51).

Thus, if they manage to merge "spontaneity" with "conscious leadership", the "subaltern classes" can increasingly "do politics" and fight for hegemony.

In the note in which Gramsci talks about the *Ordine Nuovo*, the "subaltern classes" should be understood firstly as the industrial proletariat. Gramsci's reflection here is nourished by Lenin and some sections of "What is to be done?", as well as the experience from the *Ordine Nuovo*[14]. He was probably thinking of the *biennio rosso* and the triumph of fascism when he wrote the following:

> "It is almost always the case that a "spontaneous" movement of the subaltern classes is matched by a reactionary movement of the right wing of the dominant classes, for concomitant reasons: an economic crisis, for example, produces, on the one hand, discontent among the subaltern classes and spontaneous mass movement and, on the other, conspiracies by reactionary groups, who take advantage of the objective enfeeblement of the government to attempt coups d'état" (Q3, 48, p. 51).

At the end of the note, Gramsci puts forth some arguments that talk about the articulation of the subaltern classes. He mentions the Sicilian *vespri* and adds:

> "Other examples can be drawn from all the past revolutions in which various subaltern classes took part and were ranked according to their economic positions and homogeneity. The "spontaneous" movements of the broadest popular strata make it possible for the more advanced subaltern class to come to power because of the objective enfeeblement of the state." (Q3, 48, p. 52).

I must highlight Gramsci's notion of a "more advanced subaltern class" in this note: a class who can even take power. This class is different from the marginal and spontaneous "popular strata", which moves in the terrain of "spontaneity". We use quotation

---

[14] For an in-depth analysis of this note regarding the relation leadership/spontaneity see Liguori (2011b).

marks to emphasize that, for Gramsci, there is always a spark of "consciousness".

Which conclusions can be drawn from readings the notes from *Notebook 3*? I am interested in highlighting the following one: with the term "subaltern classes", Gramsci indicates a diversified ensemble of classes, all of them characterized by not yet being hegemonic nor dominant, but highly differentiated amongst them. We go from the proletariat or classes capable of posing an hegemonic challenge and having the concrete goal of taking power, to the more marginal, peripherical and spontaneous social strata[15].

There is one last note in *Notebook 3* that we must review (one which Gramsci will retrieve in *Notebook 25*):

> "The historical unity of the ruling classes in found in the state, and their history is essentially the history of the states and the groups of states. This unity must be concrete, hence it is the outcome of the relations between the state and "civil society". For the subaltern classes, the unification does not occur, their history is intertwined with the history of "civil society", it is a disjointed segment of that history" (Q3, 90, p. 91).

Gramsci links the subaltern classes to the State and civil society in this note. The classes that remain at the level of civil society remain subaltern classes[16]. If they are not able to produce a State plan, one of organization of the national society, they cannot contend for hegemony nor pose an hegemonic challenge.

Continuing with the review of this note, we see that Gramsci invites us to study the "path of development" of the subaltern classes; a path that goes from the "more primitive stages" towards their "integral autonomy". Gramsci further pushed for the study of the differentiated reality of the subaltern classes and their political representation; that is, the study of their objective existence manifested in different levels of politization and organization in the absence of corporate or political self-consciousness. In this way, our author establishes a strong connection between a historical perspective and political theory (including one which concerns subaltern classes).

---

[15] See Baratta (2007) for some interesting observations on this matter.
[16] See Liguori (2015), particularly the chapters "Enlarged State" and "Civil Society".

For Gramsci, historical consciousness seemed a provision for the possibility of political action itself. Finally, it is important to acknowledge that subaltern classes resist or rebel, and one must take note of their resistance or rebellion. Gramsci further emphasized that the gradual conquest of a terrain for effective struggle for supremacy goes through the capacity of fighting against the adversary classes and leading the allied classes. This represents the process by which "subaltern classes" turn into an "hegemonic class".

Extension and enlargement of the word

I mentioned the title "History of the subaltern classes" above. However, what does Gramsci classify under it? For it is indeed a classification. Other than the observations from *Notebook 3* on the subaltern classes in the Roman and medieval world, the notes thus titled in the *Notebooks* are, for the most part, short bibliographic notes on intellectuals and books somehow linked to the socialist world or revolutionary moments. Gramsci did not follow the same path that he took in the notes on Lazzaretti (a reflection on the subaltern classes "on the margins of history"), nor did he reflect on the role of the non-fundamental hegemonic classes, as he started to do in the notes in *Notebook 3* regarding slaves, plebians, and the medieval proto-proletariat.

The use of the expression "subaltern classes", as well as its deviations or variations, is of greater interest to our argument. Gramsci argues that due to their subaltern character, some "social groups", must have themselves, even if temporarily, a deterministic and fatalistic ideology in order to bear the weight of a tough and seemingly dark historical situation (Q8, 205, p. 353)[17]. Furthermore, Gramsci claimed the following regarding the experience in the Soviet Union (or what he hoped happened there):

> "But when the subaltern becomes the leader and is in charge, […], there will be a revision of a whole mode of thinking because the mode of existence will have changed. The reach and the ascendancy of the "force of circumstance" will diminish. Why? Basically, because the "subaltern" who yesterday was

---

[17] I did not consider this note in my 2011 essay.

a "thing" is now no longer a "thing" but a "historical person" (Q8, 205, p.353).

And, importantly, he adds:

> "But was he ever mere "resistance", mere "thing", mere "non-responsibility"? Certainly not. That is why the ineptitude and futility of mechanical determinism, of passive and snug fatalism must be exposed at all times, without waiting for the subaltern to become leader and take charge" (Ibid).

Gramsci argues that the subaltern classes are never full passivity; there is always a seed of active resistance. That is why the reconstruction of a history that traces and values those footprints is important and has a *political* value. It is there that we find the seeds for the potential autonomy and latter hegemony of the subaltern classes. However, this will only take place in the presence of other fundamental historical conditions.

There is an interesting linguistic transition in the note Q8, 205 (written possibly in late 1931) that goes from subaltern social groups (or subaltern classes) to "the subaltern". It goes from an adjective to a noun, from plural to singular. In a certain moment of the reflections in prison, the subject to which the characteristic of "subaltern" was assigned to changes from a class or social group to a singular subject (the subaltern) — or at least there is room for that interpretation. There is evidence of a transition in such direction of *enlargement* and *extension* in the use of the word in a letter from Gramsci to his wife from August 31st, 1931:

> "I was convinced that you suffered from what psychoanalysts call "inferiority complex", which leads to a systematic repression of the strong-willed impulses, that is, our own personality, and the acceptance of a subaltern function in making decisions, even when there is a certainty of being in the right, except for having bursts of furious irritation even with matters of little importance" (Gramsci, 1995, p. 455–456)[18].

Gramsci talks about the personality traits of a singular subject in this letter. The inclination towards an individual "subaltern function" in a subject is accompanied by bursts of anger that are due to secondary aspects, which are destined to being inconclusive. It is

---

[18] I did not consider this note in the previous essay.

similar to when the subaltern masses become insurgent but later go back to their previous situation without having left their historical and substantial subalternity (particularly in the country). In a later letter, written by Gramsci to his wife, Giulia Schucht, on August 8th, 1933, we find a similar usage. Gramsci says:

> "I think that, generally speaking, you place yourself in the position of an underling rather than a leader—that is, of someone incapable of criticizing ideologies from a historical standpoint, of getting on top of them and explaining them in the light of historical needs of the past. Instead, when encountering a given world of emotions, you feel yourself alternately drawn and repelled and continue to remain within the immediate sphere of passions" (Gramsci, 1995, p. 738).

In this text, the "subaltern" refers to a person who is more culturally than socially subaltern: someone who does not know how to relate autonomously to the world views and the cultures with which he or she comes in contact with. This person develops an "hegemonic" capacity towards these cultures because he or she can't historicize nor understand them. Accordingly, the word subaltern in this letter has a cultural, partly psychological, connotation. We are close here to a particular use that the concept has acquired in recent years, which is very far from the one related to subaltern "social classes" or "social groups"[19].

This is an informal and private context, typical of a letter, which constrains the value of the Gramscian argument compared to the notes from the *Notebooks* that I mentioned above. However, it is an *indication,* a *hint* of a significant semantic change. Indeed, even with the constraints previously mentioned, this passage shows a *possibility* that we find in Gramsci's discourse itself: the dilation of the notion of "subaltern", that is, the transition of a category that emerges from the interpretation of a collective, social and class-based phenomenon to a category that refers to the *cultural* condition of subalternity in a person.

---

[19] I cannot investigate in this text the passage from "subaltern classes" to "subaltern social groups", which takes place in particular moments in the writing of the Notebooks. I will only say here that I do not believe that this indicates a paradigm shift in the Gramscian interpretation of society, but an increasing complexity of this argument.

The Notebook 25 and the Notebooks

The *Notebook 25* is a monothematic Notebook from 1934, titled *"On the margins of history (the history of subaltern social groups)"*. The Notebook is made up of eight notes and only a few pages. In it, Gramsci retrieves only part of the notes written under the title *"History of the subaltern classes"* or that had similar content. At the same time, he transcribed onto *Notebook 25* notes that did not have this title but spoke about "the subaltern" in various ways.

I will not stop to analyze this *Notebook*, both because I did it somewhere else (see Liguori, 2011a) and because I decided to analyze Gramsci's reflections on the "subaltern" from the *Notebooks*, rather than the "special notebook" dedicated to this subject. I consider this a more significant and revealing path. I will thus only turn to the title of *Notebook 25*. In truth, *"The history of the subaltern social groups"* is only the subtitle, which is in parenthesis. The title is *"On the margins of history"*[20]. Recall that Gramsci had used "subaltern classes" or similar expressions with two different meanings/connotations in the *Notebooks*[21], the first one to indicate more marginal social groups and the second one to refer to non-hegemonic social classes that fight for hegemony, which are nonetheless "fundamental classes" (slaves, plebians, modern proletariat). Thus, we see that he chose the first use of the concept for the title *Notebook 25*. In other words, he wanted to dedicate *Notebook 25* to the notes on the groups marginalized and defeated by the historical development, not to those able to pose an *hegemonic challenge*. It is clear that these groups are and could be connected to the fundamental subaltern classes; they can participate, under their leadership, in the fight for hegemony. And still, I believe that they are different from them.

In summary:

1. In Gramsci's pre-prison writings the word "subaltern" refers to the intermediate degrees of the command chain, at a

---

[20] See in particular the "anastatic edition" of the *Notebooks* coordinated by Gianni Francioni and the *Nota introduttiva al Quaderno 24* (1934–1935) found there (Francioni and Frosini, 2009).

[21] I am not considering the cultural and psychological meaning in this list, which is found in the letters mentioned above.

state-bureaucratic, military or partisan social level. It is a function that is generally considered as characteristic of the petty bourgeoisie. In the beginning of the *Notebooks*, we find the same usage of the word.
2. In *Notebook 3*, there is an emergence of the expression "subaltern classes", understood as more marginal social groups rather than non-hegemonic fundamental classes[22].
3. The title "History of the subaltern classes" first appears in *Notebook 3*. However, except for the very first notes, it does not group the most significant notes on the subject.
4. Gramsci develops the use of the concept of "subaltern" in other notes with specific references to the advanced industrial proletariat, capable of posing a challenge towards the conquest of hegemony.
5. Later on, the word is used in reference to singular subjects regarding their social location or their cultural limits. This takes us back to the interpretative wealth that Gramsci utilizes to visualize the structure/superstructure relation in a dialectical way, which in turns allows him to capture the possible ways in which subjectivities and ideologies could have incidence on the concrete historical reality (determined only "in the last instance" by the socio-economic dimension). At the same time, this does not mean that Gramsci does not connect the action of subjects with their class location and the class division of society, for Gramsci was still a Marxist during the whole period of his reflections in prison, even if it is a particularly complex and anti-economist Marxism. I must say that Gramsci provides us with wider and more comprehensive categories with the hegemon/subaltern duo compared to the classic Marxist formulation (bourgeois/proletarian). The Gramscian

---

[22] The ambivalence of the word could be considered as the basis of the controversy between Ernesto Martino and Cesare Luporini about the "popular subaltern world" in the journal *Società* between the end of the 1940s and the start of the 1950s (now in Pasquinelli, 1977). While the well-known anthropologist thought that the "subaltern classes" were those that Gramsci considered "on the margins of history", the philosopher argued that Gramsci (and the communists that followed him) would have never consider the working-class as the "subaltern class" per excellence.

categories do a better job of capturing both the social location and their subjectivity: both the structural datum and the cultural and ideological one. In this way, the category of "subaltern" enriches the traditional Marxist categories. Let us not forget that the use of the word "subaltern" found in the letters to Giulia mentioned above refers to a more extensive and fundamentally cultural-psychological use.

6. Finally, Gramsci transcribed different types of notes in which he talked about "the subaltern" to *Notebook 25*; some of them are less significant and some that are more important are missing. We must take into account that this *Notebook* was written in only a few pages, so it is possible that Gramsci did not finish the transcription as he would have wanted, or that he was not able to reformulate the matter due to external causes, as it is well-known. In any case, the importance of the category of "subaltern" is better captured by looking at the diffuse uses in the *Notebooks*, rather than the compiled notes in the "special notebook" dedicated to the subjects "on the margins of history".

Translated by María Vignau Loría

References

Baratta, G. (2007). *Antonio Gramsci in contrappunto. Dialoghi col presente*. Carocci.

Gramsci, A. (1966). "I partiti e la massa". In Gramsci, A., *Socialismo e fascismo. L'Ordine Nuovo 1921–1922*. Einaudi.

Gramsci, A. (1971). "Il nostro indirizzo sindacale". In Gramsci, A., *La costruzione del Partito Comunista 1923–1926*. Einaudi

Gramsci, A. (1984). "Il paese di Pulcinella". In Gramsci, A., *Il nostro Marx 1918–1919*, Sergio Caprioglio. Einaudi.

Gramsci, A. (1995). *Lettere dal carcere*. Sellerio

Gramsci, A. (2011). *Prison Notebooks. Volumes II and III. Edited and translated by Joseph Buttigieg*. Columbia University Press.

Hobsbawm, E.J. (1971). *Primitive Rebels*. The University Press.

Liguori, G. (2011a). "Tre accezioni di 'subalterno', in Gramsci", *Crítica Marxista*, num. 6.

Liguori, G. (2011b). "Movimenti sociali e ruolo del partito nel pensiero di Gramsci e oggi". *Critica Marxista*, num. 2.

Liguori, G. (2015). *Gramsci's Pathways*. Brill.

Liguori, G. (2013). "Los estudios Gramscianos hoy". In Modonesi, M. *Horizontes Gramscianos. Estudios en torno al pensamiento de Antonio Gramsci*. UNAM

Liguori, G. (2016). "Clases subalternas marginales y fundamentales en Gramsci". *Memoria*, 257, p. 74–79

Modonesi, M. (2014). *Subalternity, Antagonism, Autonomy. Constructing the Political Subject*. Pluto Press.

Francioni G. and Frosini F. (2009). "Nota introduttiva al Quaderno 24 (1934-1935)". In Gramsci, A., *Quaderni del carcere. Edizioni anastatica dei manoscritti*. Edited by G. Francioni. Biblioteca Treccani-L'Unione Sarda.

Pasquinelli, C. (1977). *Antropologia culturale e questione meridionale. Ernesto De Martino e il dibattito sul mondo popolare subalterno negli anni 1948–1955*. La Nuova Italia.

Chapter 3

Thompson and the experience of class

María Vignau Loría

> "Class is defined by men
> as they live their own history,
> and, in the end,
> this is its only definition"
> E.P. Thompson[1]

Introduction

Many Marxist studies that deal with the concept of social class start by revising the classical postulates and the ensuing debates, turning eventually to the introduction of a new concept, the enunciation of a particular conceptual property or the enumeration of criticisms and condemnations. Edward Palmer Thompson did not follow this path. Instead, the English author created a concept of social class based on his historiographical work. In this way, Thompson's sharp historical exploration allowed him to sketch a concept of social class that was profoundly innovative and highly provocative. At the same time, and following his own convictions, Thompson never developed a systematic theory on his concept of class, nor did he worry about placing it at the center of the Marxist debates. Most of the theoretical debates on his work were done by other scholars; activists and Marxists who recovered the Thompsonian conceptualization.

The concept of social class developed by Thompson is linked to many aspects of his life and political thought which, for the most part, are the correlate of his research and the position that he adopted regarding his own scholarly production. Thompson had an academic career that was characterized by his profound critique to the academy, his disagreement with academic consensus and

---

[1] Preface to *The making of the English working class* (Thompson, 1966, p. 11).

"specialists", and his rejection to dogmas and theoretical trends and fads[2]. He was a professor to those who were at the margins of the academic elites[3], and he even left his post as a professor at the University of Warwick due to his disagreement with the practices and the course of the academic world[4]. At the same time, his life was always marked by strong political commitments: he was one of the main voices of the peace movement that called for nuclear disarmament and he placed those activities above and beyond academic ones. He was also a defender of civil rights in England, and a stark critical of Stalinism and "real socialism", which led him to abandon the Communist Party after the Soviet invasion of Hungary (Illades, 2008, p. 17-27). As a historian and Marxist, Thompson espoused a profoundly critical and oftentimes polemic discourse; he criticized both the theoretical orthodoxies in Marxism and the ideological assumptions that he believed were their foundation. His studies were highly unusual in the context of the English Marxist historiography of the time. Thompson's work spanned very different areas: historical and literary essays published in several compilations, the acclaimed biographies of William Morris and William Blake, and studies on social history in the 18th century which recovered the practices and customs of popular culture (Thompson, 2000, p. 9). As Carlos Illiades argued, "[Thompson's] theoretical and methodological reflections reveal his position regarding his own discipline of study and the products of knowledge" (Illades, 2008, p. 13).

---

[2] This is revealed, for instance, in the following extract of one of his essays: "I have to say honestly, without any sense of particular criticism, or of any large theoretical statement, that I'm less and less interested in Marxism as a Theoretical System. I'm neither pro nor anti so much as bored with some of the argument that goes on. [...] I feel happier with the term historical materialism. And also with the sense that ideas and values are situated in a material context, and material needs are situated in a context of norms and expectations, and one turns around this many-sided societal object of investigation." (Thompson, 1995, p. 301-302).

[3] Thompson himself mentions that he tutored adults for many years, teaching at nights to workers, union members and white-collar people (Illades, 2008, p. 19).

[4] According to Thompson, the University of Warwick was changing its direction to serve the interests of companies and industries. He mentions that "what was wrong was the whole concept and structure of the University. The ideals of academic excellence and the pursuit of knowledge had to be reasserted over the aims of the "Business University" (Thompson, 1970).

His most famous work, *The making of the English working class*, which was first published in 1963, is considered a highly influential and revolutionary work of Marxist historiography. It is important to clarify that the "emergence" of the working class in England was a phenomenon that had been studied from other perspectives (or "prevailing orthodoxies", as Thompson would call them). Firstly, it was studied by an approach based on economic history that considered workers as passive victims of the transformations brought about by the industrial revolution and free markets. Secondly, by an economic empirical perspective that saw workers as labor force statistics in an emerging economic system. Thirdly, by a vision that exalted the working class, those who directed and headed revolts and rebellions, as "pioneers of the Welfare State". In stark contrast to all these approaches, Thompson turned his attention to the "poor stockinger, the Luddite cropper, the 'obsolete' hand-loom weaver, the 'utopian' artisan" (Thompson, 1966, p. 12), and thus reconstructed the history of the working class as the protagonist of the economic and social process, rather than its victim.

According to Thompson himself, the purpose of his book was twofold. His first goal was to make *social history* of the *people* that lived during a period of profound transformations in England (1780–1832). From a historiographical point of view, Thompson tried to distance himself from traditional historiography, that is, one which "reads history in the light of subsequent preoccupations, and not as in fact it occurred" (Thompson, 1966, p. 12). He made an effort to track and reconstruct the everyday actions and agency of working people that "contributed, by conscious efforts, to the making of history" (Ibid). In an essay titled *Folklore, anthropology and social history* (Thompson, 1977) Thompson confessed to a certain eclecticism in his work as a historian due to his focus on concerns that were usually associated with anthropology. He likewise mentioned the difficulties he faced when doing research for *The making of the English working class* regarding the "recovery and understanding of popular culture and ritual" (Thompson, 1977, p. 247). Those difficulties were not only nor necessarily academic. They were instead political hardships, given that, at the time, "popular culture" was regarded as conservative by most Marxist historians[5]. For the English author, however, the study of folklore, tradition, custom, and "the plebeian consciousness and forms of protest of the eighteen century" should lead to questions about "past states of consciousness and the texturing of social and domestic relationships", not just to questions about change that are posed from the present. Additionally, Thompson argued that these studies should focus on the "immense supporting cast" which, rather than "attendants upon the process" (as they are regarded in traditional historiography), is the element that allows us to truly understand a particular epoch[6] (Thompson, 1977).

A second purpose of the book, according to Thompson, was to contribute to the understanding of one of the main preoccupations of the Marxist agenda: *the formation of social classes*. He deliberately argued against the Marxist conceptualizations rooted in economism and schematism, which used a simplified and deterministic formula and thus reduced the emergence of the working class to changes in the modes of production and the productive forces, specifically to the appearance of the steam machine and the new worker-employer relationship. Thompson argued that most historians did recognize that "the outstanding fact of the period between 1790 and 1830 is the formation of the 'working class'" (Thompson, 1966, p. 194); indeed, in 1832, "the working-class presence was the most significant

---

[5] On this subject, Thompson mentioned that "the rise of Fascism led to an identification of folk studies with deeply reactionary or racist ideology. And even on less sensitive historical ground, an interest in customary behavior tended to be the prerogative of the more conservative historian. For custom is, by its nature, conservative. Historians of the Left tended to be interested in innovative, rationalizing movements, whether Puritan sects or early trade unions [...]" (Thompson, 1977, p. 250).

[6] Thompson talks about women to exemplify this point. He mentions that "[...] there are whole periods in history in which an entire sex has been neglected by historians, because women are rarely seen as prime agents in political, military or even economic life. If we are concerned with being, then the exclusion of women would reduce history to futility. We cannot understand the agrarian system of small cultivators without examining inheritance practices, dowry, and (where appropriate) the familial development cycle. And these practices rest, in turn, upon the obligations and reciprocities of kinship, whose maintenance and observation will often be found to be the peculiar responsibility of the women (Thompson, 1977, p. 251).

factor in British political life" (Ibid, p. 12). But many see its emergence as "the spontaneous generation of the factory-system" (Ibid, p. 194). Those who see it that way, he said, "have lost a sense of the whole process – the whole political and social context of the period" (Ibid, p. 196). Thompson's study goes beyond the documentation of the material conditions of exploitation of English workers; it tracks the *different facets of the experiences* of the people who lived through those conditions and experienced a diverse set class relationships – from Luddite crises in small workshops, Owenite organizations, Cartists movements, the radical Jacobinism of artisans, etc. Furthermore, Thompson tracked other political and social forces that were part of this process given that, in his own words, "the making of the working class is a fact of political and cultural, as much as of economic, history" (Ibid, p. 194)[7]. And he added a final warning: the new productive relations and working conditions brought about by the Industrial Revolution – in Marxist language, the objective determinations of the capitalist structure – did not operate as an external force upon "some nondescript undifferentiated raw material of humanity" that would later be transformed into "the working class". They were imposed instead upon men and women with particular traditions, customs, religions, ways of thinking and behaving; in other words, men and women with particular histories[8]. Accordingly, the identification of those elements of particular history become necessary to understand the process of class formation in a holistic way.

As I mentioned, Thompson's work does not include a revision of the different theories on social class that were part of the Marxist production of the time. From his own disciplinary trench and with a very particular way of approaching his object of study, Thompson

---

[7] For instance, Thompson argued that the political counter-revolution of 1972-1832 had as much influence as the steam-engine "upon the shaping of class-consciousness and institutions of the working-class" (Thompson, 1966, p. 197). This counter-revolution, which referred to the political oppression in the face of Jacobin radicalism that arrived to England following the French Revolution, led to "growing self-consciousness and wider aspirations" for working people (Ibid, p. 198).

[8] Ellen Meiksins Wood identified this idea as the "basic theoretical and methodological principle of Thompson's whole historical project" (Wood, 1995, p. 92).

traced the process of class formation between 1780 and 1832 to a "multitude of individuals with a multitude of experiences" (Thompson, 1966, p. 11). Consequently, the examination of Thompson's work is not easy nor simple, in his own words, it is more a "group of studies, on related themes, rather than a consecutive narrative" (Ibid, p. 12). However, the implications of his work and historiographic studies would influence an entire generation of Marxists regarding the concept of social class and the importance of the notion of *experience*. Furthermore, and together with other English thinkers, he would set the stage for a Marxist tradition whose object of study would be the cultural expressions of the material and objective constraints/determinations of the economic structures.

The concept of social class

E.P. Thompson understands by class:

> "[...] an historical phenomenon, unifying a number of disparate and seemingly unconnected events, both in the raw material of experience and in consciousness. I emphasize that it is an historical phenomenon. I do not see class as a "structure", nor even as a "category", but as something which in fact happens (and can be shown to have happened) in human relationships". (Thompson, 1966, p. 10).

Envisioned like this, that is, as a "historical phenomenon", class can only be understood and studied as a *process*. A process in which, in Thompson's words, class "did not rise like the sun at an appointed time", but "was present at its own making". This "process-like" conceptualization of class has two implications that must be analyzed here.

First, as a historical phenomenon and as a process, class can only be observed through an extended period of time. Let's consider Thompson's words:

> "If we stop history at a given point, then there are no classes but simply a multitude of individuals with a multitude of experiences. But if we watch these men over an adequate period of social change, we observe patterns in their relationships, their ideas, and their institutions." (Thompson, 1966, p. 11).

This is why Thompson considered it necessary to explore 52 years of history in order to find those "patterns" that allowed him to talk about the "working class". Following this argument, we could say that class never fully "is", but is "made by being", and it is only through diachronic analyses that it is possible to study and understand it. In his essay, *The peculiarities of the English,* Thompson argued that sociologists that stop the "time machine" in order to locate a class by using "a good deal of conceptual huffing and puffing" can only find "a multitude of people with different occupations, incomes, status-hierarchies, and the rest" (Thompson, 1965, p. 357). The definition of class, according to Thompson, "can only be made in the medium of time—that is, action and reaction, change and conflict" (Thompson, 1965, p. 357).

Second, Thompson considered that any analysis on social classes must always be embodied "in real people and in a real context" (1966, p. 9). He constantly criticized the abstract Marxist theories that lacked serious analyses of "real contexts". We can assume that our author was thinking, for the most part, about the theoricism of Louis Althusser and his concept of class, which was rooted almost exclusively in an ensemble of abstract formulations that had not been empirically tested (Thompson, 1995).

Let us move to the second part of the definition. Class is not a "structure" nor a "category", but "something that in fact happens in human relationships". This idea is intimately connected to what I mentioned above: understanding class as a process implies that it can only be truly grasped within a specific context. But it goes even further: class is not something that is attributed to a group of individuals from the outside, whether it is academia or politics. Class is a "happening"[9], it is something that "happens in human relationships", in other words, class is lived and experimented.

To better understand this idea, it is necessary to reconstruct another important element of Thompson's conceptualization. According to our author:

---

[9] In his essay, *The peculiarities of the English*, Thompson argues that "class itself is not a thing, it is a happening" (Thompson, 1965, p. 357).

> "class happens when some men, as a result of common experiences (inherited or shared), feel and articulate the identity of their interests as between themselves, and as against other men whose interests are different from (and usually opposed to) theirs" (Thompson, 1966, p. 9).

Let us first analyze the idea of *experience*, given that it is a central notion in Thompson's thought. From the pages of *The making of the English working class* we can discern the following: people live under determined relations of production and objective conditions "into which men are born—or enter involuntarily" (Thompson, 1966, p. 9). It is by *experiencing* these objective conditions (relations of exploitation and domination) that some people identify common interests between themselves (and antagonist to others), which leads to corresponding forms of organization and, in turn, to their "identification" as a class.

This is evident in Thompson's historiographical work. The author recognizes two simultaneous processes as the *objective conditions of the relations of production*. The first one is found in the new forms of exploitation (new forms of organization and distribution of labor) in agriculture, domestic industries, new factories and mines. The second one refers to the circumstances encountered by workers: factory workers that faced terrible working conditions, farmers that lost communal rights, artisans and manufacturers that turned into salaried workers, amongst others (Thompson, 1966, p. 198-212)[10]. But the analysis does not end there. It is nurtured by stories that explore the *experience* of such exploitation and such conditions; an experience which contributed to the "social and cultural cohesion of the exploited" (Ibid, p. 198). Accordingly, it is a cohesion that first arises from the sharing of experiences, and later on, from the identification of shared interests—for instance, workers that find themselves all in favor of direct cooperative action, or against the utilization of machines in manual workshops. At the same time, workers identify the masters as "others", and they see them "not as an aggregate of individuals, but as a class" (Ibid, p.

---

[10] The address of the "Journeyman Cotton Spinner" to the of public of strike-bound Manchester does a great job of illustrating these circumstances (Thompson, 1966, p. 199-202).

206)[11]. The last stage of this process would then be the rising of the "political expression and cultural expression of working-class consciousness" (Ibid, p. 212), which is observed in "class" organizations that demand rights, plan strikes or affiliate to union-type institutions.

Following Thompson, Ellen Meiksins Wood referred to "class situations" to capture the distribution of people in "determinative productive relations". As she mentioned, Thompson considered this "objective distribution" into class situations as the "beginning, not the end, of class formation" (Wood, 1995, p. 81). Individuals distributed in class situations *experience* those objective material conditions and, through that experience, they identify *class interests* and, eventually, they *think and act in class ways*. Thompson calls this phenomenon a *disposition to behave as a class*, referring to the ways in which "a very loosely defined body of people" shares interests, social experiences, traditions and value-systems, which allows them to "define themselves in their actions and in their consciousness in relation to other groups of people in class ways" (Thompson, 1965, p. 357). Following this argument, when Thompson referred to "class struggle without class" (Thompson, 1978), he was precisely talking about how, before there is a presence of mature class formations, people behave in class ways, they share "dispositions to behave as a class", and they adopt class interests—common between themselves but antagonistic and in conflict with those of the other class.

Thompson's notion of "behaving as a class", which accompanies class interests, paved the way for a an understanding of class as a cultural formation, not just a social one[12]. In this way, Thompson, together with other thinkers like Raymond Williams or Stuart Hall, inaugurated a perspective within Marxism that regards

---

[11] Thompson mentions that, by identifying the masters as a class, the worker recognizes that "'they' deny him political rights. If there is a trade recession, 'they' cut his wages. If trade improved, he had to tight 'them' and their state to obtain any share in the improvement. If food was plentiful 'they' profited from it. If it was scarce, some of 'them' profited more. 'They' conspired, not in this or that fact alone, but in the essential exploitive relationship within which all the facts are validated" (Thompson, 1966, p. 206–207).

[12] "Class is a social and cultural formation (often finding institutional expression)" (Thompson, 1965, p. 357).

cultural manifestations as places of expression of both class exploitation, and class resistance.

There is another element of Thompson's concept of social class that I must highlight: his emphasis that class is *relationship*. If we bring back a fragment of the passage mentioned above, in which he argued that "men feel and articulate the identity of their interests as between themselves, and as against other men whose interests are different from (and usually opposed to) theirs", we realize that our author placed an emphasis on the fact that classes always exist *in relation to one another*. The same happens when he mentioned that groups define themselves "in their actions and in their consciousness in relation to other groups of people in class ways". In other words, the identification of the group with antagonistic interests is a necessary step in the identification of oneself as part of the other group.

Finally, it is important to mention that we are not dealing with just any kind of social relation: this is a relation of exploitation, domination, conflict and struggle. For Ellen Meiksins Wood, Thompson's notion of "class as a relationship" not only implies a relationship between different classes, but a relationship between the members of the same class, which is clearly evident in the ways in which *experience* leads to conducts, value-systems, traditions and similar interests (Wood, 1995).

Let us move to the idea of class consciousness. According to Thompson, "class-consciousness is the way in which these [class] experiences are handled in cultural terms: embodied in traditions, value-systems, ideas and institutional forms" (Thompson, 1966 p. 10). We can thus see how, despite the analytical distinction, class and class consciousness arise and occur at the same moment. The identification of similar and antagonistic interests, as well as the coming to think and value in class ways, are key elements in the emergence of both class consciousness and the process of class formation[13]. Additionally, although Thompson admitted that class experience is "largely determined by the productive relations into

---

[13] According to Thompson, "we cannot put 'class' here and 'class consciousness' there, as two separate entities, the one sequential upon the other, since both must be taken together — the experience of determination, and the 'handling of this in conscious ways" (Thompson 1995, p. 143).

which men are born—or enter involuntarily" (Thompson, 1966, p. 9), class consciousness is not similarly determined. Thompson argued that there is certainly a certain *logic* to class consciousness (in that we can expect certain outcomes), but it never arises in "just the same way" (Ibid, p. 10).

There is a final note I would like to make regarding Thompson's notion of class consciousness, and that is his harsh critique to what he calls "theory of substitution" (Thompson, 1966 p. 10). With this concept, our author referred to the Marxists that attributed certain characteristics to the working class based on a formula retrieved from Marx's writings and applied relatively automatically: there is a working class constituted by a certain number of people who stand in a determined relation to the means of production and, from there, it is possible to know what class consciousness and interests they "should have". Thompson calls it "theory of substitution" because class is conceived from ideals, forgetting what it "is" in favor of what "it should be". Accordingly, supporters of this perspective think of "the party, sect or theorist, who disclose class consciousness" (Ibid, p. 10) as the ones that will end with the "cultural lags and distortions" that hinder the evolution of class "as it ought to be".

These arguments and assertions allow us to really glimpse Thompson's commitment to the historical interpretation of "real subjects". He tried to understand and give a voice to common people who may have had a "backward-looking hostility to new industrialism" or "outlandish communitarian ideals", while reductionist Marxist perspectives, which mainly saw "distortions", "lags" or "nuisance" in the cultural superstructure, regarded their "backward attitudes" as obstacles to the formation of a revolutionary working class (Thompson, 1966, p. 10–12).

The legacy of Thompson's concept of social class

"I wish only to indicate that, for its author,
the major theses of [The making of...] still stand as hypotheses which,
in their turn, must never be petrified into orthodoxies"
E. P. Thompson[14]

---

[14] Preface to the 1980 edition of *The making of the English working class*.

Perry Anderson once claimed that, despite his refusal to systematize his work at a theoretical or conceptual level, Thompson made "deliberate and focused contributions to theory: no other Marxist historian has taken such pains to confront and explore, without insinuation or circumlocution, difficult conceptual questions in the pursuit of their research" (Anderson, 1980, p. 2). It is thus that, through his work in historiography, his essays, prologues, conferences and other contributions, Thompson fashioned a concept of social class that would influence and inspire Marxist scholars everywhere and even transcend the Marxist tradition itself.

In these next lines, I will highlight five specific contributions of Thompson's concept of social class in order to fully display the originality, reach and implications of his work and studies.

First, we have Thompson's idea that class is a process, that is, the fact that "we cannot understand class unless we see it as a social and cultural formation, arising from processes which can only be studied as they work themselves out over a considerable historical period" (Thompson, 1966, p. 11). Assertions such as these were questioned when they crossed the borders of the historical discipline and the historiographical method, since both Marxists and sociologists study existing class formations that, as such, cannot be subjected to diachronic analysis. However, by criticizing those that study the social world by "stopping the time machine" or "freezing theory", Thompson did not necessarily deny the possibility of a synchronic study of class. Instead, he gave us two warnings: first, class will always be an unfinished process, a process that is still happening. Second, a study of class at a particular point in time must not forget that it is dealing with a socio-historical process. In other words, that an a-historical analysis that does not consider that there are historically structured processes underlying empirical data, is condemned to failure.

Second, we have Thompson's arguments regarding the study of class in real contexts and with real peoples. This posture is firmly outlined in *The poverty of theory* and the brutal attack to Althusser's epistemology which, according to Thompson, "exhibits a radical indifference towards primary data" (Anderson, 1980, p. 5) and leaves out any sense of historical explanation (Thompson, 1995, p. 44).

According to Thompson, theory should never be dissociated from the practice from which it originated. This applies particularly to Marxist theory, whose homeland "remains where it has always been, the real human object, in all its manifestations (past and present): which object however, cannot be known in one theoretical *coup d'oeil* (as though Theory could sallow reality in one gulp)" (Thompson, 1965, p. 60). Thus, Thompson pushed back against all those who use a "self-generating conceptual universe which imposes its own ideality upon the phenomena of material and social existence, rather than engaging in continual dialogue with these" (Ibid, p. 18).

Third, Thompson's concept of social class pertains to a *social relation*, not to structural locations (expressed as the distribution of individuals in systems of stratification or hierarchy) nor to a "simple" relation to the means of productions, as could be understood by some schools of thought within Marxism. As Wood argues, "the focus is on the social relation itself, the dynamic of the relation between appropriators and producers, the contradictions and conflicts which account for social and historical processes" (Wood, 1995, p. 71). Indeed, to talk about social class is to talk about social relations of exploitation and domination.

Fourth, it is important to highlight Thompson's acknowledgement that social classes exist in the *cultural domain*, not as alienation, but as the expression of the objective and material determinations. In other words, Thompson claims that the behaviors, practices, customs, value-systems and all other cultural elements that are found in the "disposition to behave as a class" are key objects of study in the process of class formation.

This acknowledgement was highly criticized by many scholars from other Marxist perspectives, including Perry Anderson, whose arguments are synthetized in his book *Arguments within English Marxism*. In this text, Anderson analyses Thompson's work according to what he calls "its four main problems: the character of historical inquiry, the role of human agency in history, the nature and fate of Marxism, and the phenomenon of Stalinism" (Anderson, 1980, p. 3). Beyond the fruitful exchange of this dialogue, I am interested in what Anderson said about Thompson's concept of social class.

According to Anderson, Thompson proposed "a definition of class that is far too voluntarist and subjectivist" (Anderson 1980, p. 40), because "it is not the structural transformations—economic, political and demographic—which are the objects of his inquiry, but rather their precipitates in the subjective experience of those who lived through these 'terrible years'" (Ibid, p. 39). Anderson takes up similar critiques made by Gerald A. Cohen, where both of them reclaim Marx's thesis that "a person's class is established by nothing but his objective place in the network of ownership relations [...] His consciousness, culture and politics do not enter the *definition* of his class position" (Ibid: 40). In Anderson's view, the "whole thrust" of Thompson's argument "is still to detach class form its objective anchorage in determinate relations of production, and identify it with subjective consciousness or culture" (Ibid, p. 42).

It is possible to understand Anderson's harsh criticism of Thompson's work, particularly as it relates to Thompson's emphasis on certain cultural expressions or forms of consciousness and his relative inattention to the relations of production. However, I think that Thompson's acknowledgement of these "cultural" manifestations as an important part of the process of class formation does not mean that he defines social class based on culture or consciousness, nor does it mean that he disregards the objective determinations of the relations of production. Let us remember that Thompson argued that all cultural and conscious expressions are firmly conditioned by the objective situations of exploitation and domination, anchored in turn in relations of production, and it is only through their *subjectivation through experience* that they move to the cultural domain. The preeminence, if we want to call it that, is in the "class situations" in which people are distributed into (where men are born or enter involuntarily). As Wood mentions, "class consciousness is possible because 'objective' class situations already exist" (Wood, 1995, p. 83) Thompson's acuity lies in making visible elements of social class that are not strictly in the domain of the relations of production, and in drawing our attention to the fact that classes exist when there are no mature and evident class institutions and organizations.

Finally, I would like to highlight Thompson's notion of experience as a key element of the conceptual development of class. This notion allows us to understand class formation as a process of *collective subjectivation of the objective determinants in the relations of production*; an active process that, in the words of our author, "owes as much to agency as to conditioning" (Thompson, 1966, p. 9). Additionally, beyond its explicative potential in the process of class formation, the notion of experience sheds light in the way in which Thompson understood the dialectical relation between "social being and consciousness", between "agency and structure", between the "objective determinants and the subjective formation". For Thompson, experience is both a "middle term" and a "dialogue" between the objective determinants and the subjective initiative, a dialogue that, above all, goes in both directions (Thompson, 1995, p. 12)[15].

Thus, an important element in Thompson's criticisms to structural Marxism in general, and to Althusser in particular, developed in *The poverty of theory* responded precisely to affirmations that claim that "history is a process without a subject", that "structures must be analyzed and individual wills should be cast aside", and that "the very notion of human agency is no more than the semblance of a problem for bourgeois ideology" (Thompson, 1995, p. 119). In this way, while Althusser thinks that history does not have a subject, but rather structures that determine them, Thompson's notion of experience allows us to understand how "structure is transmuted into process, and the subject re-enters into history" (Ibid, p. 229). The notion of experience allows us to understand the dialectics between "agency" and "process". It allows us to grasp, in Thompson's words, "the crucial ambivalence of our human presence in our own history, part-subjects, part-objects, the voluntary agents of our own involuntary determinations" (Thompson, 1995, p. 119).

---

[15] Thompson argues in The poverty of theory that "if social being is not an inert table which cannot refute a philosopher with its legs, then neither is social consciousness a passive recipient of 'reflections' of that table" (Thompson, 1995, p. 12).

References

Anderson, P. (1980). *Arguments within English Marxism*. NLB

Illades, C. (2008). *Thompson*. Universidad Autónoma Metropolitana

Thompson, E. P. (1965). The peculiarities of the English. *The Socialist Register*, 2.

Thompson, E. P. (1966 [1963]). *The making of the English working class*. Vintage Books

Thompson, E. P. (1970). *Warwick University Ltd: Industry, Management and the Universities*. Penguin.

Thompson, E. P. (1977). Folklore, anthropology and social history. *The Indian historical review*, vol 3 (2): 247-266

Thompson, E. P. (1978). Eighteen century English society: class struggle without class?. *Social History*, 3 (2):133-165

Thompson, E. P. (1995). *The poverty of theory. Or an orrery of errors*. Merlin Press

Thompson, E. P. (1995). Agenda for radical history. *Critical Inquiry*, 21 (2): 229-304

Wood, E. M. (1983). El concepto de clase social. In E. Thompson. *Cuadernos Políticos*, 36: 87-106.

Wood, E. M. (1995). "Class as process and relationship". In *Democracy against capitalism. Renewing historical materialism*. Cambridge University Press

Chapter 4

Poulantzas and the structuration of classes

María Vignau Loría

> "Instead of suppressing differences and thus
> inevitably choosing to brush fundamental problems under the carpet,
> I have preferred to dwell on them,
> in so far as criticism alone can advance Marxist theory"
> Nicos Poulantzas[1]

Introduction

Nicos Poulantzas was a Marxist scholar and sociologist who studied in France under the tutelage of one of the most important proponents of structural Marxism: Louis Althusser. This led to his adoption of many of the premises and propositions of this school of thought, as well as his recognition as one of its most representative figures. Despite his structuralist bent, Poulantzas' work, published within a period of ten years (between 1968 and 1978), aimed to fill a gap in the Marxist tradition regarding "the political", which he defined as the juridico-political superstructure of the state (as well as its role in the reproduction of capitalism and its relationship to other regional structures), and "politics", which are the political class practices (Poulantzas, 1973, p. 37). Hence, many of his contributions to the understanding of the concept of social class and class conflict in Marxism are aimed at explaining "its repercussions on the field of the political" (Ibid, p. 57).

Before fully delving into his conceptualization of social class, I will briefly explore Poulantzas' interpretation of two key Marxist propositions, which are necessary to understand his concept of class.

First on this list is the distinction between *mode of production* and *social formation*. A mode of production is an "abstract-formal

---

[1] Foreword to *Classes in contemporary capitalism* (1975, p. 11).

object which does not exist in the strong sense in reality" (Poulantzas, 1973, p. 15); in other words, it is an abstract construction that is defined by the type of relations of production that characterize it; for instance, the slave, feudal or capitalist mode of production. On the other hand, a social formation is "a real-concrete object and so always original because it is singular" (Ibid), in other words, historically determined social wholes. Accordingly, there are as many social formations as there are real-concrete objects of study. Poulantzas uses the example of France under Louis Bonaparte (as studied by Marx), but we can also think about France in the seventies, or 21st century France; each one with their own particularities and specificities as real, concrete and singular objects. This distinction is important because while abstract-formal objects (modes of production) don't exist as such, they are the "condition of knowledge of real-concrete objects" (Ibid, p. 13). This distinction is similarly present in many of the concepts that allow us to understand the capitalist system; the "capitalist State" does not exist as such, but only as "historically determined capitalist formations" (Ibid, p. 17). The same happens with social classes, which "only exist in the form of class struggle and practices" in particular social formations (Poulantzas, 1975, p. 14)[2]. Additionally, one of the main characteristics of a social formation is that it presents "a particular combination, a specific overlapping, of several 'pure' modes of production" (Poulantzas, 1973, p. 15), in other words, it combines elements of different modes of production, such as, for example, the presence of certain features of feudal social organization within in a capitalist market economy. According to Poulantzas, these combinations in particular social formations are marked by the dominance of one of the

---

[2] It is important to include here Poulantzas' thoughts on abstract-formal concepts and their application. According to our author, "the most concrete concepts, those which lead to knowledge of a social formation at a definite time in its development, are not, any more than real-concrete objects, the raw material of the process of thought; neither are they deduced from the most abstract concepts, or subsumed under these latter, simply particularizing their generality. They are the result of a work of theoretical elaboration which operates on information, notions, etc., by means of the most abstract concepts, in order to produce the most concrete concepts leading to the knowledge of real, concrete, singular objects" (Poulantzas, 1973, p. 13).

modes of production over the others. Finally, it is important to note that modes of production and social formations are not only defined by "the economic" (relations of production), but rather, by "a specific combination of various structures and practices which, in combination, appear as so many instances or levels, i.e. as so many regional structures of this mode" (Poulantzas, 1973, p. 13).

This takes us to the second element in the list, which is the identification of *regional instances* or *regional structures* in a mode of production or social formation. Poulantzas argues that a mode of production is constituted by the articulation of three regional instances: the economic, the political, and the ideological[3]. Further, these instances "are not already constituted essences, which then enter into external relations with each other, according to the scheme of base and superstructure—a schema which, if taken literally, is ambiguous. The articulation peculiar to the totality of a mode of production governs the constitution of its regional instances" (1973, p. 17). According to our author, the political and ideological regional instances possess relative autonomy and their own efficacy, even when they are *determined in the last instance* by the economic (Ibid, p. 14)[4]. This is a delicate passage, because Poulantzas' understanding of the relation of "economic determination", which has been the object of endless debates in the Marxist tradition, is key to the construction of his entire conceptual apparatus. He acknowledges that there is a determination by the economic (the relations of production and the productive forces) if conceptualized as "a *complex whole* dominated, in the last instance, by the economic" (Ibid, p. 14). However, he rejects "certain interpretations of Marxism" which construe a "circular and expressive totality, founded on a central-

---

[3] Let's briefly review the definition of each regional instance or structure. The economic instance is defined as the "relations of production and the productive forces", the political instance as "the institutionalized power of the state" (Poulantzas, 1973, p. 42), and the ideological instance as "an ensemble of material practices", rather than "a system of ideas" or a "coherent discourse" (Poulantzas, 1975, p. 17).

[4] The questions regarding this relative autonomy and efficacy lie at the very center of the debate "voluntarism and economism". On the one side, there are those who only think about the "dynamic-historical-political" aspect, and on the other, those who invalidate the specificity of the political (Poulantzas, 1973, p. 38).

subject instance which is the foundational category and the principle of genesis, and of which the other instances, 'total parts', constitute only the phenomenal expression" (Ibid, p. 14). According to Poulanztas, these interpretations negate the possibility of studying the regional instances (particularly the political) because they conceptualize the relation to the economic structure as one of "linear causality, or expressive mediation, or analogical correlation". Instead, in Poulantzas words, this is "a type of relation in which the structure in dominance governs the very constitution (the nature) of the regional structures, by assigning them their place and by distributing functions to them" (Ibid, p. 14). He goes even further by making a distinction between "determination in the last instance" and "dominant role". In this way, even when the economic is always determinant in the last instance, the dominant role in the structure can be held by the political or the ideological. This is possible because "the economic is in fact determinant only in so far as it attributes the dominant role to one instance or another, in so far as it regulates the shift of dominance which results from the decentration of the instances" (Ibid, p. 14)[5]. The conceptualization of "regional instances" is a key component of Poulantzas' theoretical approach because, as we will see, social classes are not only determined by the economic instance, but by the political and ideological ones as well.

I will analyze Poulantzas' concept of social class by reviewing two of his most important works. The first one, *Political power and social classes* (1973), which came out in France in 1968, is an exhaustive and rigorous study of the capitalist State. According to Poulantzas, any study of the State would be impossible without an analysis of the role that social classes and class struggle play in its reproduction. The second one, *Classes in contemporary capitalism* (1975), was published in 1974 in France. It contains a series of essays in which Poulantzas analyzes social classes and the state apparatuses in

---

[5] To illustrate this point, Poulantzas brings back Marx's point in which he argues that in the feudal mode of production, the ideological instance (and its religious form) played the dominant role, a situation that was only made possible by the functioning of the economic determination in the last instance (Poulantzas, 1973, p. 15).

imperialist/monopolist capitalism (which our author considered as the "present phase" of capitalism) and which are based on the theories and framework developed in his earlier work. The essays on social classes are dedicated to studies of the bourgeoisie (in Poulantzas' words, "the working class' enemy") and the petty bourgeoisie ("the working class' potential allies"). Our author is particularly concerned with the study of these two classes because he considers that they have been neglected by Marxist theory and, as he argues, "today it is more than ever the case that an essential component of revolutionary strategy consists in knowing the enemy well, and in being able to establish correct alliances" (Poulantzas 1975, p. 9).

The concept of social class

Let us start with a review of Poulanztas' arguments in *Political power and social classes* (1973) since this is where we find the foundations of his conceptualization and theory of social classes. His analysis of the concept of class begins with a careful study of the works by Marx, Engels and Lenin (although throughout his text he also brought up other authors and schools of thought, even making occasional references to "the functionalist school" in contemporary sociology). Poulantzas' interest in developing a definition of class that fit well in the field of "the political" and "politics" brought him close to the political works of these authors, particularly the studies of specific political conjunctures and historical formations.

Poulantzas review of "the problem of the theoretical status of classes" starts with Marx's distinction between the "economic struggle" and "political struggle" of classes, in which there are three levels or moments (1973, p. 58). The first one refers to the economic struggle between workers and capitalists. This struggle between "individuals/agents of production" does not yet reveal class relations, rather, it is characterized by the presence of an "incoherent mass" in a "common situation and with common interests", as defined by Marx in both the *Communist Manifesto* and *The Poverty of Philosophy*. The second level refers to what has been usually called "class-in-itself", that is, when the clashes between different agents of production progressively become collisions between two classes upon the identification of shared economic interests. The third level would then be "class-for-itself", in other words, political class struggle, or class organized politically. According to Poulantzas, this analytical distinction has been interpreted wrongly since its declaration.

Poulantzas groups these erroneous interpretations into two big categories. The first one, the "historicist interpretation", conceptualizes social classes with a "historico-genetic" understanding, which takes the three levels as if they were a historiography of the process of class formation[6]. In other words, this interpretation confuses theoretical-analytical levels with stages of class formation: first there is an undifferentiated mass of workers, which then becomes a class-in-itself, and later on becomes a class-for-itself (1973, p. 60)[7]. Furthermore, these works, according to Poulantzas, not only confuse theoretical levels with historical moments, but perceive "social classes as the subjects of history" (1973, p. 60). In other words, they think of social actors as creators and transformers of structures, which is a voluntarist conception that, for Poulantzas, is unacceptable in a theory of social classes[8].

The second erroneous interpretation is the "economist" one, which only recognizes the existence of classes at the level of relations of production, reducing them to the "the position of agents in

---

[6] Poulantzas notes that "the different levels of analysis of social relations, described by Marx as moments of historical genesis, ought *here* to be considered as a *theoretical process* of the construction of the *concept* of class" (Poulantzas, 1973, p. 75, emphasis by the author).

[7] Poulantzas identifies two currents within the historicist group. The first one is that in which "class is conceived as the subject of history, as the factor of genetic production and of transformations of the structures of a social formation. Lukács is the typical representative of this historicist interpretation of class and class-consciousness" (Poulantzas, 1973, p. 60). The second current is related to the functionalist interpretations of Marx, where structures and social classes "are grasped in a relation of structure to function, of synchrony to diachrony" (Ibid, p. 61); this diachrony is expressed in the historicist interpretation that "men make their own history".

[8] According to Poulantzas, this interpretation "fails to recognize two essential facts: firstly, that the agents of production, for example the wage-earners and the capitalist [...], are considered by Marx as the supports or bearers of an ensemble of structures; secondly, that social classes are never theoretically conceived by Marx as the genetic origin of structures, inasmuch as the problem concerns the definition of the concept of class" (1973, p. 62).

the labor process and to their relation to the means of production" (Ibid, p. 62). Poulantzas argued that Marx did not only talk about classes in reference to the economic structure, but in reference to the ensemble of the structures of a mode of production or social formation, "and to the relations which are maintained there by the different levels" (Ibid, p. 63); social classes can thus be identified both in the political instance or the ideological one[9]. This "economist interpretation" should not be confused with the *economic determination/domination in the last instance* that was previously discussed; the latter is still accurate despite the acknowledgment that the economic structure is not the only player in the definition of social classes.

I will now carefully examine the definition provided by Poulantzas in this work. According to our author:

> "A social class is a concept which shows the effects of the ensemble of structures, of the matrix of a mode of production or of a social formation on the agents which constitute its supports: this concept reveals the effects of the global structure in the field of social relations" (Poulantzas, 1973, p. 67)".

Let us start with the first part of the definition: "a social class is a concept that shows the effects of *the ensemble of structures* [...] on the agents which constitute its supports...". This is where the distinction between the regional instances or regional structures in a mode of production or social formation grows in importance. As I mentioned, Poulantzas argues that social classes are not exclusively defined as a consequence or effect of the economic structure, but as an effect of the articulation of all of the structures. There is another important caveat to point out here: this is not an effect of the economic over the other structural effects (political and ideological), but a

---

[9] Poulantzas argues here that "[the economic determination of social classes] by no means implies that [it] is sufficient for the construction of the Marxist concept of social class, any more than the specific treatment of the economic instance of the CMP [Capitalist Mode of Production] in Capital lessens the importance of the other instances for the scientific examination of this mode" (Poulantzas, 1973, p. 57). He further argues that "a social class can be identified either at the economic level, at the political level, or at the ideological level, and can thus be located with regard to a particular instance" (Ibid, p. 63).

global effect of the ensemble of the structures and the relations between them[10].

There is another key component in this first part of the definition: "social class is a concept that shows the *effects* of the ensemble of structures[...]". In order to avoid possible misinterpretations, Poulantzas clearly states what he means by "effects": "we should not, of course, take the term 'effects' in a chronological sense; this would be to make a genesis back to the front. I mean by 'effects' the existence of the determination of structures in social classes" (Poulantzas, 1973, p. 68). This type of statements allows us to see why Poulanztas is undeniably a proponent of structural Marxism. Indeed, while our author does not think that classes are *economically determined*, he does think that they are *structurally determined*. We saw glimpses of this structuralist tendency in his criticism to the historicist interpretations of Marx's theory of classes: Poulantzas stresses that classes are not the genetic origin of structures; they are not the subject of history[11].

Let us move on to the last part of this first sentence: "social class is a concept that shows the effects of the ensemble of structures *on the agents which constitute its supports*". This argument complements what has been said before: "agents" are precisely "agents of

---

[10] "It must be stated at once that social classes do not present themselves as the effect of one particular structural level on another structural level: i.e., as the effect of the economic structure on the political or ideological structures; hence they do not manifest themselves inside the structure, but entirely as the *global effect of the structures in the field of social relations*, which, in class societies, themselves involve the distribution of agents/supports to social classes: and they do this to the extent that the social classes determine the place of agents/supports in relation to the structures of a mode of production and a social formation. The confusion of these fields has a name in the history of Marxist thought: it is anthropologism of the subject" (Poulantzas, 1973, p. 64).

[11] It is important to note here that Poulantzas and Althusser had different stances regarding both structuralism and historicism. This is particularly evident in some passages found in *Political Power and Social Classes*, in which Poulantzas enhances his analysis of "the political" — including discussions on political power, the characteristics of the capitalist State, the hegemony of the dominant classes — with Gramsci's arguments. Thus, despite his claim that Gramsci had a "historicist conception of dialectical materialism", or that there were "after-effects of historicism" in his work, Poulantzas readily acknowledges his "very enlightening" contributions and his "amazing acuteness" (Poulantzas, 1973, p. 195).

production"; they are the "*supports* or *bearers* of an ensemble of structures" (Poulantzas, 1973, p. 62). In other words, individuals are bearers of structures, not their genesis.

I will finish this detailed examination by looking at the second statement in the definition: "... this concept reveals the effects of the global structure *in the field of social relations*". According to Poulantzas, class is not a partial or regional structure within the global structure of a mode of production or a social formation (such as the State, for instance), but a concept that "denotes social relations" (1973, p. 68). Neither are classes an "empirical concrete" that express a concept[12]. In other words, it is possible for the effect of structures to generate other structures (again, the State is a good example), but that is not the case for social class, because there is no "theoretical homogeneity" between a concept that denotes structures and one that denotes social relations[13].

It follows then that a reference to social relations is always a reference to class relations[14]. Furthermore, class relations are not only social relations of production (the economic instance), but juridico-political "social" relations and ideological "social" relations. While neither the juridico-political superstructure of the State nor the ideological structure are social classes, they have as their effect

---

[12] According to Poulantzas, "social classes are not, in fact, an 'empirical thing' of which the structures are the concept. They denote social relations, social ensembles: but they are the concept of them, in the same way as the concepts of capital, of wage-labor, and of surplus value constitute concepts of structures, of relations of production" (1973, p. 67).

[13] Poulantzas argues that the Marxist "economist interpretation" of social classes originated from a failure to properly distinguish between structures and social relations. These interpretations use the terms "relations of production" and "social relations of production" without any distinction, while, according to our author, they are quite different. The first one refers to "the relations of the agents of production and the means of labor", while the second ones are "relations among agents of production distributed in social classes, i.e. class relations" (1973: 64 - 65). This is a tricky and rather problematic passage, as Poulantzas claims that despite the fact that Marx himself used these terms without distinction, "it is only by an attentive reading of his texts that we can discover the difference between the realities covered in these concepts" (1973, p. 64).

[14] "If class is indeed a concept, it does not designate a reality which can be placed in the structures: it designates the effect of an ensemble of given structures, an ensemble which determines social relations as class relations" (Poulantzas, 1973, p. 68).

social relations that distribute agents-bearers into social classes. To clarify this argument, Poulantzas puts forward a distinction similar to the one that differentiates between "determination in-the-last-instance" and "dominant role" when talking about regional structures in a mode of production or social formation. According to our author, the determination in-the-last-instance of the economic class struggle in the field of social relations can be "reflected by a displacement of the dominant role to another level of class struggle — political or ideological struggle" (1973, p. 69)[15].

Finally, it is important to highlight that Poulantzas' concept of social class finds them in the domain of social relations as "practices"[16] and as "struggle" despite their structural determination. We see this in our author's claim that "social classes can be conceived only as class practices [and] these practices exist in opposition which, in their unity, constitute the field of the class struggle" (1973, p. 86). In other words, Poulantzas conceptualizes social classes as relations of conflict, of opposition, of contradiction.

There is a final proposition from *Political Power and Social Classes* that I will review here, which is related to Poulantzas' remarks on the "number of classes". In a "pure" mode of production, the effect of the ensemble of structures on the agents is reflected in a distinction between two classes: wage-earners and capitalists (proletariat and bourgeoisie). On the other hand, in a historically determined social formation (which articulates features of different "pure" modes of production), the effects of the concrete combination of different instances of different modes of production give rise to "a whole series of phenomena of splitting, dissolution and fusion of classes", including the appearance of other categories (1973, p. 73). In this way, Poulantzas rejects the interpretations that attribute

---

[15] Delving deeper into this argument, Poulantzas claims that "the way in which classes are related to the relations of production and to the economic structure has the determining role in the constitution of social classes: this role provides precise evidence of the constant determination-in-the-last-instance by the economic element in the structures, as reflected in social relations" (1973, p. 69).

[16] "Classes always denote class *practices, and these practices are not structures*: political practice cannot be identified with the superstructure of the state, nor economic practice with relations of production" (Poulantzas, 1973, p. 69, emphasis by the author).

the difference in the number of classes to a plurality of criteria in their definition. The definition of classes, he claims, is exactly the same. Instead, the difference comes from the presence of different modes of production in a historically determined social formation, as well as the specific ways in which the instances or regional structures are concretely combined and articulated. He further claims that Marx's lack of specificity regarding social formations and modes of production when talking about social classes led to confusing and ambiguous interpretations.

Let us further examine the problem of social classes in a historically determined social formation that is, the "splitting, dissolution and fusion of classes" mentioned above. Poulantzas claims that it can't be assumed that the classes that result from the theoretical examination of a "pure" mode of production exist concretely as distinct classes in a particular conjuncture. Rather, we see the emergence of "certain distinct classes", which our author calls "autonomous fractions of classes", and which appear in a social formation as "dissolved and fused with other classes" (1973, p. 77). These autonomous fractions of classes are important in the analysis of social formations because they can become "social forces" that play an essential role in specific conjunctures. In order to identify the presence of a "distinct character of class" in a social formation—in other words, to identify an existing autonomous and distinct fraction—it is necessary that "the relation to the relations of production, the place in the process of production, is reflected on the other levels by *pertinent effects*" (Ibid, p. 79). For instance, the political organization of a class has pertinent effects in other non-economic levels[17]. There

---

[17] We step here into a rather obscure passage in the definition of an autonomous fraction or distinct class. According to Poulantzas, the criterion to decipher their existence as a social force in a formation is their presence in other (non-economic) levels as reflected by "pertinent effects". Our author defines them as "the fact that the reflection of the place in the process of production on the other levels constitutes a new element which cannot be inserted in the typical framework which these levels would present without this element" (1973, p. 79), which could be interpreted as an important change in the political or ideological structures, or a significant novelty in the field of political or ideological struggle. The problem lies precisely in how to determine which changes or novelties are important or significant, that is, what is the "typical form of the levels" that changes when introducing a new element that "depends on the concrete

are two examples that illustrate this last point: first, Marx's analysis of the small-holding peasants as a distinct class in the *The Eighteenth Brumaire*[18]. A second example is Poulantzas' own analysis of the petty bourgeoisie in his work *Social classes in contemporary capitalism*.

I will now turn to Poulantzas' second work, *Classes in contemporary capitalism* (1975). As mentioned before, this is not a systematic study of social classes but a collection of essays in which our author studies the relationship between the state in its current phase (imperialist/monopolist capitalism), the state apparatuses and social classes. While our author mentions that "certain analysis and formulations" from his previous works were "rectified in this text", he maintains the basic propositions (Poulantzas, 1975, p. 11). What makes this work different is that Poulantzas faces the challenge of analyzing social classes empirically, specifically the bourgeoisie and the petty bourgeoisie.

The first element that I will examine here is a reformulation of the importance of class practices and class struggle. According to Poulantzas, "social classes involve in one and the same process both class contradictions and class struggle; social classes do no firstly exist as such, and only then enter into a class struggle" (1975, p. 14). Rejecting once again the notion that class struggle only exists as "class-for-itself", Poulantzas argues that "there is no need for there to be 'class consciousness' or autonomous political organizations for the class struggle to take place, and to take place in very domain of social reality" (Ibid, p. 17). Our author is thus able to analyze

---

conjuncture of a concrete historical situation" (1973, p. 81). We are thus confronted with a rather circular theoretical argument: the autonomous fractions of classes are defined by their "presence" in the other instances, which is in turn identified by "pertinent effects", which are observed when they fall outside the "typical framework" of these instances.

[18] Let us briefly examine this example. According to Poulantzas, the small-holding peasants in the concrete conjuncture examined by Marx "constitute precisely a distinct class to the extent that their place in the process of production is reflected in this concrete conjuncture, at the level of political structures, by the historical phenomenon of Bonapartism which would not have existed without the small peasant farmers" (1973, p. 79). Thus, "the economic existence of the small holding peasants is reflected, on the political level, by the pertinent effects constituted by the particular form of the state of Bonapartism as a historical phenomenon" (Ibid, emphasis by the author).

social classes in their contradictions and oppositions in the political field without abandoning his stance regarding their structural determination (and thus avoiding voluntarist interpretations as well).

Another important formulation is the distinction regarding "class places" and "class positions". According to Poulantzas, the structural determination of classes "designates certain objective *places* occupied by the social agents in the social division of labor" (1975, p. 14). The "place of class" corresponds to the structural determination of class, which is expressed in class relations and class practices. On the other hand, "class positions" refer to the positions occupied by classes in a social formation's concrete conjunction. The importance of this distinction lies in the relationship between the two: according to our author, it is possible for a class to have a "position" (in the conjuncture) that does not correspond to its "place" (in the structure). Poulantzas exemplifies this argument with the "labor aristocracy"; their structural determination makes them part of the working-class but they adopt the interests and positions of the bourgeoisie in particular conjunctures. This distinction further supports the claim that the structural determination of class cannot be reduced to class positions—to do so "would be tantamount to abandoning the objective determination of the places of social classes for a 'relational' ideology of 'social movements'" (1975, p. 16). Here we see once again Poulantzas' emphasis on the distinction between the structural determination of classes and their political expression in specific conjunctures. Finally, echoing the arguments from his previous work, Poulantzas reminds us that the structural "class places" are not solely determined by the economic structure (and later expressed in the political and ideological domain), but a determination of the *ensemble of structures*. Similarly, "class positions" in the conjuncture are expressed not only in economic class struggle, but in political and ideological class struggle as well.

A third important formulation from this text has to do with the arguments that support the empirical analysis of social classes. Poulantzas claims that "the classes of a social formation cannot be 'deduced', in their concrete struggle, from an abstract analysis of the modes and forms of production which are present in it, for this is not how they are found in a social formation" (1975, p. 23). This is related to his claim that social classes are only found in the domain of social relations as practices and struggle: in order to do an empirical analysis of classes, they need to be "materialized" in concrete ways in a specific social formation. It follows then that the study of political class struggle and political class practices are a good approach to study classes in concrete, historically determined, social formations.

Finally, in this text, Poulantzas makes a direct contrast between the Marxist concept of social class and the sociological conceptualizations that define classes as "empirical groups" based on the characteristics of the agents that compose them[19]. According to Poulantzas, the principal characteristic of an analysis of social classes is that of "their places in the class struggle" (1975, p. 17) — these places, as we know, are structurally determined. Thus, our author heavily criticizes those who are concerned with the class membership of particular individuals, with the establishment of empirical boundaries of social groups, or the conceptualization of the relationship between groups as "social inequalities"[20].

---

[19] In Poulantzas' words, "classes are not empirical groups of individuals, social groups, that are composed by simple addition" (1975, p. 17).

[20] Following these arguments, Poulantzas censures those interpretations that define classes based on wages, income, benefits, and other such criteria. Instead, we should see these indicators as "indexes" of class determination, while different forms of social inequalities are the effects of "class barriers". In Poulantzas' words, "social inequalities are only the effect, on the agents, of the social classes, i.e. of the objective places they occupy, which can only disappear with the abolition of the division of society into classes. In a word, class society is not a matter of some inequality of 'opportunity; between 'individuals', a notion which implies that there is opportunity and that this depends wholly (por almost so) on the individuals, in the sense that the most capable and the best individuals can always rise above their 'social milieu'" (1975, p. 17). Additionally, our author strongly criticizes the theories (ideologies, in his words) of social stratification in sociology. Poulantzas argues that they conceptualize social classes as a partial form of stratification within a general hierarchy. In our author's words, "the principal question about 'social stratification', or even about its origin, is that of the 'circulation' or 'mobility' of individuals between strata. However, it is clear that, even on the absurd assumption that from one day to the next, or even from one generation to the next, the bourgeoisie would all take the places of workers and vice versa, nothing fundamental about capitalism would be changed, since the places of bourgeoisie and proletariat would still be there, and this is the principal aspect of the reproduction of capitalist relations" (1975, p. 33).

The implications of Poulantzas' work

> "No individual theoretical worker or militant,
> nor even a group of theorists or militants,
> is in a position to elaborate a [systematic theory of social classes].
> This could only be a product of the working class' own organizations
> of class struggle"
> Nicos Poulantzas[21]

The work of Nicos Poulantzas can be considered as one of the most ambitious efforts to build a systematic theory social classes within the Marxist tradition which, despite the accusations of "excessive theoretism" (partly because of his association to Althusser), aimed to explain concrete historical conjunctures.

Poulantzas' work on social classes was characterized by his attempt to locate them in the field of "the political" without falling into what he considered "voluntarist extremes". In other words, it is an extraordinary and rigorous effort to study classes' political practices and struggles, while still fixing its definition in some of the "toughest" elements of Marxism, such as structural and economic determinism. Hence, while Poulantzas fully incorporated structural determination in his theoretical apparatus, he still found a way to unfold the concept of class into political struggle through ingenious theoretical arguments such as the identification of regional structures or instances with relative autonomy, the differentiation between a mode of production and a social formation, and the distinction between the level of structures and the level of social relations.

Poulantzas' focus on *the political* and *politics* in his conceptualization of social classes does not mean that their "effective existence" at this level is conditioned to the acquisition of class consciousness; Poulantzas believes that such arguments, identified mostly with Lukacs, Korsch and the Theoretical Leftism of the Third International, over-politicize Marxism under a historicist interpretation of a process "acted" by the class-subject (Poulantzas, 1975, p. 76–77). In other words, the distinction between economic class struggle and political class struggle—indeed, the distinction between class' relation to the regional economic structure and the

---

[21] Foreword to *Classes in Contemporary Capitalism* (1975, p. 9)

regional political structure—does not mean that classes only fully (effectively) exist in the political field. This is why Poulantzas rejected Marx's distinction between class-in-itself and class-for-itself as a "Hegelian reminiscence" that not only failed to provide clarity to the notion of social class, but fostered historicist interpretations that mistook the status and role of "the political" as the genesis of class struggle, rather than as a particular level of social relations (i.e. as political class struggle).

I will end this chapter by summarizing what I think are the three most distinctive elements and contributions of this author's concept of social class to the Marxist debate and beyond.

Firstly, the claim that social classes are neither partial structures nor empirical things, but practices and struggles located in the domain of social relations. This argument makes for a comparatively flexible concept in which classes, although *structurally determined*, can be studied in the fields of production, politics or ideology through social practices, contradictions, organizations, struggles, interests, etc.

A second element to reiterate is the conceptualization of social classes as an effect of the ensemble of the economic, political and ideological structures. This claim comprises a critique to both Marxist historicism (or any interpretation that rejects structural determination and magnifies the role and weight of the subject) and Marxist economism (or any interpretation that formulates class determination as an effect of the economic structure alone). In this sense, and together with the distinction between dominant role and determination, Poulantzas' stance emerges as a sort of relative middle ground that acknowledges the importance of the political-ideological superstructure while maintaining an anchor in the economic base in-the-last-instance.

Finally, I want to highlight Poulantzas' distinction between an abstract analysis of social classes in a mode of production and a concrete study of classes in a historically determined social formation. We see in this structuralist scholar a clear concern to work with and for concrete conjunctures, which is even more obvious in his analyses of the bourgeoisie and the petty bourgeoisie in *Classes in contemporary capitalism*.

In this way, the conceptualization of social class by Nicos Poulantzas bears several groundbreaking elements in regards to the construction of a novel theoretical framework. We thus have a rigorous and creative theorist that recuperates the classical elements of Marxist thought and Marxist analysis and brings forth innovative tools to deepen the critique to capitalism and the system of social classes.

Excursus: Ralph Miliband and social classes in the capitalist state

As mentioned before, Poulantzas' work stands out for his concern over "the political" and "politics", both in his arguments regarding social classes and even more in regards to his work on the capitalist state. In this second field, his reflections and theories on the nature and role of the state in contemporary capitalism were the object of a fruitful debate with the English Marxist Ralph Miliband, particularly around the problems of the autonomy of the state, its nature as a "structure" or an "instrument", and its relation to the dominant classes[22].

Miliband argued that the Marxist tradition lacked systematic theorizations that treated "politics" as a specific phenomenon, which he argued was notable given Marxists' own engagement in political struggles. For some Marxists, politics were an omnipresent component that, in its ubiquity, lacked a specific character. For others, politics were so determined and conditioned by the economic structure that they lacked any substantial degree of autonomy (Miliband, 1977). With this in mind, Miliband aimed to reconstruct a Marxist political theory and a Marxist political analysis on the basis of a theory of the state. This particular approach is due to Miliband's claim that "in the politics of Marxism, there is no

---

[22] For a glimpse of the debate between Poulantzas and Miliband on the capitalist State see the articles in the *New Left Review*, "The Problem of the capitalist State" (Poulantzas, 1969), "The capitalist State: reply to Nicos Poulantzas" (Miliband, 1970), "Poulantzas and the capitalist State" (Miliband, 1973) and "The capitalist State: a reply to Miliband and Laclau" (Poulantzas, 1976).

institution that is nearly as important as the state" (1977, p. 66)[23]. A state which, additionally, has always been "an essential means of class domination" (Ibid, p. 67).

This particular theoretical—and indeed, political—agenda is responsible for the ties between Miliband's reflections around social classes and his theory of the state. Thus, while he did not systematically work on the concept of social class, it was inevitable that, throughout his intellectual career, the English Marxist would reflect on the role of social classes and class struggle in relation to the state. For instance, he thought about "dominant classes" based on their relationship to the "state power". Additionally, the "working class" was defined on the basis of the concept of *domination*, in which the state plays a fundamental role.

Let's begin with Miliband's arguments on the relationship between the dominant classes and the State[24]. The English author considered that this theorization was particularly problematic in the Marxist tradition: on the one hand, the "class-reductionist tendencies" in Marxism obscured the self-regarding and independent role of the state, on the other, the "state-reductionist bias" gave the idea of the "primacy of politics" too much leeway (Miliband, 1983, p. 65). In an attempt to avoid both forms of reductionism, Miliband conceptualized the relationship between the dominant classes and the state as a *"partnership between two different, separate forces"* (Ibid). With this approach, he acknowledged both the space in which political and state action operates, and the constraints that the capitalist context places upon the state. Additionally, this association was envisioned as a dynamic partnership, one that was constantly modified by different circumstances, particularly class struggle.

---

[23] Miliband believed that the state had a crucial role in Marxist political analysis; this is clear in the introduction to his work about the state in capitalist society. He writes that "more than ever before now, men now live in the shadow of the state. What they want to achieve, individually or in groups, now mainly depends on the state's sanction and support. But since that sanction and support are not bestowed indiscriminately, they must, ever more directly, seek to influence and shape the state's power and purpose, or try to appropriate it altogether. It is for the state's attention, or for its control, that men compete: and it is against the state that beat the waves of social conflict (Miliband, 1969, p. 1).

[24] Miliband used "ruling class", "dominant class" or "capitalist class" indistinctly to refer to the bourgeoisie.

Following this formulation, Miliband reevaluated the problem of the autonomy of the state—which he considered central to any and all reflections of Marxist political theory—in relation to class struggle. In frank disagreement with Poulantzas' approach, which Miliband claimed would lead to "structural super-determinism" or "structural abstractionism" (Miliband, 1973, p. 85), he argued that the degree of autonomy of a given state depended on the extent to which class struggle and the pressures from below challenged the hegemony of the dominant class. Accordingly, in cases in which the dominant class has economic, political, cultural and ideological hegemony, the state would have very little autonomy since it would also be subjected to the hegemony and class power of the capitalist class. On the other hand, in cases in which the hegemony of the dominant class is continuously challenged—in other words, in times in which class struggle is more intense—the state would have much more substantial autonomy (Miliband, 1983, p. 61).

The relationship between state power and the power of the dominant classes is thus very complex and fraught with constant tensions. On that note, Miliband criticized Marxist approaches that assumed that "class power is automatically translated into state power" (Miliband, 1977, p. 67), in other words, that the ownership and control of the material and mental means of production is "automatically translated" into the control and direction of the state. According to Miliband, there are two problems with this assumption. First, the ruling class has many factions and divisions. Second, class interests and national interests do not always "precisely coincide". This complexity can be seen in the reforms and regulations enacted by capitalist states that are contrary to the interests of the dominant classes, or by the presence of "governments of the left" that have come to power in capitalist states[25].

Let's now move on to Miliband's thoughts on social classes. While he recognized the undeniable importance of exploitation in

---

[25] Miliband believed that the only case in which there was a rupture in the partnership between a left-wing government and the dominant class was Salvador Allende's government in Chile. However, the government was not capable of forging a new partnership with the subordinate classes, and thus its autonomy became its own "death warrant" (Miliband, 1983, p. 66).

class analysis—understood as the extraction of surplus value in the relation between the owners of capital and the labor force–, Miliband constantly highlighted the concept of *domination*, and its corollary, class *subordination*, as the pillars of Marxist politics and class analysis (Miliband, 1977). Exploitation, argued Miliband, is of crucial importance, but only made possible by domination (Miliband, 1987, p. 328)[26].

Miliband argued that anchoring the concept of social class on the notion of domination "widens the framework within which class relations and class struggle are considered" (Miliband, 1987, p. 328). By encompassing the broader social and political context, this approach corrects for the economism tendencies promoted by the primacy of exploitation in the definition of classes, class struggle and class analysis. To this he added the fact that "the state is an essential means of class domination" (Miliband, 1977, p. 67). Additionally, Miliband argued that the focus of domination in class analysis makes the concept of class more flexible in regards to the classical formulation based on "the ownership of the means of production". A dominant class is thus constituted by "virtue of its effective control over three main sources of domination: the means of production, the means of the state and coercion, and the means of communication and consent" (Miliband, 1987, p. 329). There are two elements that I want to highlight here. First, the emphasis on the "effective control" of the means of domination implies that the *ownership* of either of these means is not an essential requirement to *exercise* the control of the "main sources of power in capitalist society: corporate power and state power" (Ibid, p. 329). Second, the inclusion of other sources of domination in the definition of social classes grants them a relatively more heterogenous character that, in turn, makes for a rather more flexible empirical-concrete characterization of classes in post-industrial capitalist societies.

---

[26] This idea is in direct opposition to Erik Olin Wright's arguments that claim that a "domination-centered" concept of social class slides into a "multiple oppression" approach, in which "class, then, becomes just one of many oppressions, with no particular centrality to social and historical analysis" (Wright, 1985, p. 57).

In this way, the dominant class is far from homogenous. It includes more than the owners of corporations, but those who control the strategic and commanding positions in the state system, and those that own or control the means of communication in a society. Similarly, the notion of "control of the means" (as opposed to "ownership of the means") identifies as members of the dominant class the growing numbers of managers, who control important facets of business life without owning them. Miliband argues that the three dominant class fractions often share interests and thus usually protect each other and the advancement of their common purposes. However, there are also differences and conflicts amongst them, which is why the previously mentioned *partnership* between the economic elite and the state—in other words, the political elite—is so important in Miliband's understanding of class struggle and class analysis.

The subordinate class—the working class in the classical formulation in Marxism—is an extremely heterogenous class across occupations, qualifications, gender, races, ethnicities, ideologies and religions: this class is not only comprised by industrial and manual workers, but by the majority the world's population whose source of income is the sale of their labor-power. Miliband is aware here of the many problems posed by a definition of the working class as "wage-earners"; first and foremost, the working class would include managers, directors and other high-rank executive personnel that live off their salaries. Instead, the English Marxist defines working class as "part of the 'collective laborer' which produces surplus value, from a position of subordination, at the lower ends of the income scale, and also at the lower ends of what might be called the 'scale of regard'" (Miliband, 1977, p. 24). Finally, the recognition of differences within the subordinate class acknowledges the importance of other forms of oppression that have not always been brought to attention in Marxist studies of class, such as sexism, racism or nationalism (a challenge and harsh critique that has been posed to Marxist class analysis by activists and scholars alike). In Miliband's words, "social beings are complex and contradictory entities in which different identities coexist", and the recognition of these identities does not reduce the importance of class as an intrinsic and "*decisive* part of their 'social being'" (Miliband, 1987, p. 343).

The final element that I would like to highlight in this brief *excursus* is related to Miliband's reflections on class consciousness. On the one hand, the English author identified a distinction between the objective dimension of social classes—defined, as mentioned before, as a function of the effective control of the means of domination—and a subjective dimension that is related to Marx's arguments regarding the political organization of a class. While Miliband considered that class consciousness had a decisive importance in Marxist politics, particularly at a strategic level, he did not develop a systematic theory on the transit from the "objective dimension" of class to a "subjective" one, nor did he explore the process of formation of class consciousness. Rather than looking closely at the role of the subordinate classes in their emancipation, his concern with the absence of class consciousness in the working class led him to focus on the mechanisms of domination, particularly those related to the state and the dominant classes.

In sum, Ralph Miliband developed a concept of social class that took off from his work and reflections on the state in capitalist society. By conceptualizing the state as an essential means of class domination and, at the same time, as transformed by class struggle, Miliband came up with a concept of social class that placed the interpretative keys in the domains of conflict, domination and political practice and struggle.

References

Connell, R.W. (1992). A critique of the Althusserian Approach to Class. In A. Giddens & D. Held (Eds.). *Classes, Power and Conflict. Classical and contemporary debates*. Macmillan

Miliband, R. (1969). *The State in capitalist society*. Basic Books Ink Publishers.

Miliband R. (1970). The capitalist State: reply to Nicos Poulantzas. *New Left Review* 59: 53–60.

Miliband, R. (1973). Poulantzas and the capitalist State. *New Left Review* 82: 83–92.

Miliband, R. (1977). *Marxism and Politics*. Oxford University Press.

Miliband, R. (1983). State Power and class interest. *New Left Review* 138: 57–68.

Miliband, R. (1987). Class Analysis. In A. Giddens (Ed.), *Social Theory, Today*. Polity Press

Poulantzas, N. (1969). The problem of the capitalist State. *New Left Review* 58: 67–78.

Poulantzas, N. (1973). *Political Power and Social Classes*. Verso

Poulantzas, N. (1975). *Classes in Contemporary Capitalism*. NLB.

Poulantzas, N. (1976). The capitalist State: A reply to Miliband and Laclau. *New Left Review* 95: 63–83.

Poulantzas, N. (1979). *Fascism and Dictatorship*. Verso Editions.

Wright, E. O. (1985). *Classes*. Verso

Chapter 5

Wright and class in Analytical Marxism

María Vignau Loría

> "Abstract concepts are to be evaluated
> not only for their logical presuppositions and coherence,
> but for their usefulness in more concrete investigations"
> Erik Olin Wright[1]

Introduction

In a time in which scholars increasingly abandoned the "classical" notion of social class that originated from Marx's work, the work of American sociologist Erik Olin Wright stands out for his contribution of new and renewed elements to the study of contemporary social classes.

Together with the rigor and commitment that characterized his intellectual endeavors, his work is distinguished by five elements that have made his conceptualization of class one of the most innovate and original contributions to the contemporary Marxist debate. First, it is firmly rooted within Marxism. Second, its debates are situated in a particular academic discipline: sociology. Third, it prioritizes empirical analysis, using for the most part quantitative approaches and methodologies. Fourth, many aspects of his work are embedded in the academic Marxism[2] of the United States[3].

---

[1] *Interrogating Inequality: essays on class analysis, socialism and Marxism* (Wright, 1994, p. 65).

[2] I would like to briefly mention Wright's thoughts on "academic Marxism". He argued that this term "is often used pejoratively, suggesting politically disengaged careerism and intellectual opportunism". By using it, he "does not mean to impugn the motives of Marxists who work in the University. [...] Rather, this expression reflects the historical reality that in the present period, Marxism is most rigorously articulated and elaborated within academic disciplines rather than within revolutionary movements as such" (Wright, 1994, p. 179).

[3] Wright argued that many Marxists are suspicious of "academic Marxists", particularly of those in the United States, where there is an absence of a cohesive mass socialist movement and a revolutionary working-class political party. He

Consequently, it establishes dialogues with American schools of thought like the stratification tradition[4]. Fifth, Wright's work is anchored in the "Analytical Marxism" school of thought (or as his founders call it, "*Non-Bullshit Marxism Group*"[5]).

Wright's adherence to Analytical Marxism demands an examination of the premises that characterize this school of thought, since many of the particularities of his analyses and concept of class respond to the core principles of this group.

Analytical Marxism emerged in the final years of the 1970s as a consequence of Marxism's entrance into the universities of "developed capitalist democracies" in the aftermath of the social movements of the 1960s (Wright, 1994, p. 179). This school of thought aimed to reconstruct Marxism's explicative scope and potential, following the conviction that the political project of emancipation that lies at the heart of central Marxist categories such as class, exploitation, historical materialism and capitalism has both theoretical and political validity. The group incorporated a very diverse set of members, including thinkers such as G.A. Cohen, John Roemer, Jon Elster, Adam Prezeworski, Philippe Van Parjs and Robert Van der Veen among others. They all worked on a diverse set of subjects,

---

himself mentioned that his work "has been informed by social and political events, [rather than] forged in direct engagement with popular struggles". He further claims that while he does not know whether his work has been benefited or suffered from the circumstances of its production, it has not stopped him from maintaining "the kind of self-reflective stance that might minimize the negative effects of these material conditions on [his] work" (Wright, 1985, p. 3).

[4] In general terms, Wright identified three sociological schools of thought that deal with class analysis. First, the stratification tradition, which identifies class with individual attributes and life conditions. Second, the Weberian tradition, which focuses on the way in which individuals' social position gives them control over economic resources of various sorts while excluding others from access to those resources (social closure). Third, the Marxist tradition, which defines class based on mechanisms of exploitation and domination, that is, "economic positions that give some people control over the lives and activities of others" (Wright, 2015, p. 3). While Wright's theoretical conversations with non-Marxist thinkers will not be explored in this chapter, it is important to take note of his interest in establishing dialogues and building bridges with different theoretical traditions. In these conversations, our author was particularly interested in highlighting the particularities—and superiority, in his view—of a Marxist conceptualization and understanding of social class.

[5] According to Wright, this is the less high-blown name of the group (Wright, 1994, p. 14).

"including such things as class structure, the theory of history, the problem of ideology, normative political theory, basic concepts of Marxian economics, social democracy and electoral politics, economic crisis, trade unions and the state" (Wright, 1994, p. 180), and had quite diverse political positions.

Notwithstanding this diversity, Wright argued that there are four principles or "commitments" that characterize and distinguish Analytical Marxism, justifying its designation as a "distinct school" of contemporary Marxist thought[6]. These principles are (Wright, 1994, p. 181-182):

1. *"A commitment to conventional scientific norms in the elaboration of theory and the conduct of research"*. This principle implies that Analytical Marxists think that Marxism should "aspire to the status of genuine social science", in other words, it should work under the scientific standards that produce empirical research that is tied to theoretical models. It is important to note here that aspiring to scientificity is not the same as working under the assumptions of positivism[7].

2. *"An emphasis in the importance of systematic conceptualization, particularly of concepts that are at the core of Marxist theory"*. This principle refers to the explicit purpose of Analytical Marxists to work systematically in the analytical and logical coherence of Marxist concepts, in many cases re-conceptualizing the classical formulations and theories.

3. *"A concern with a relatively fine-grained specification of the septs in the theoretical arguments liking concepts, whether the arguments can be about causal processes in the construction of explanatory theories or about logical connections in the construction of*

---

[6] Wright was aware of the critiques that Analytical Marxism received from other Marxist thinkers. He argued that, while there's always been a debate regarding whom the "true" Marxists are within the Marxist tradition, it is more constructive to recognize that "Marxism is not a unified theory with well-defined boundaries, but a family of theories united by a common terrain of debate and questions" (Wright, 1994, p. 178).

[7] Wright did not specify what analytical Marxism understand by "science". Instead, he argued that most Analytical Marxists adopt a realist view of science, that is, a view that "science attempts to identify the mechanisms which generate the empirical phenomena we experience in the world" (Wright, 1994, p. 183).

normative theories. This commitment to elaborating the details of arguments is reflected in one of the hallmarks of Analytical Marxism: the use of explicit, systematic models of the processes being studied". Analytical Marxists used abstract models with different levels of formalization that go from game theory models to causal models. According to Wright, the elaboration of explicit models allowed researchers to get at the heart of the complexity of social phenomena by identifying the mechanisms involved, the way that they work, and the connections between them. He further argued that this formal articulation gave analyses a clarity that often escaped the work of many historical and empirical Marxist researchers[8].

4. *"The importance accorded to the intentional action of individuals within both explanatory and normative theories"*. This is the most controversial principle of Analytical Marxism, since it recognizes some of its members' closeness to rational choice theory, including the assumptions of rational actor models, methodological individualism or the use of game theory. While Wright acknowledges the importance of the relationship between "individual decisions and social processes" and thinks that "social theory should incorporate a concern with conscious choice", he is aware that social processes can't be reduced to problems of individual intentionality. Thus, he does not adopt all the principles of methodological individualism, and he recognizes the limits in the explicative potential of formal models of rational actors[9].

---

[8] Wright argued that "it is generally the case that lurking in the weeds behind every informal causal explanation is a tacit formal model. All explanatory theories contain certain assumptions, claims about how the various mechanisms fit together. The difference between Analytical Marxists do and what many historical and empirical researchers do, then, may be basically a question of the extent to which they are prepared to put their cards on the table and articulate the causal models in their theories" (Wright, 1994, p. 187).

[9] To further explore the relationship between Marxism and rational choice theory, including that which has been called "Rational Choice Marxism" (identified particularly with Jon Elster's work), see Elster's *Making Sense of Marx* (1985) or *Marxism, functionalism and game theory* (1982).

These principles have been subjected to harsh criticism and controversy within the Marxist tradition. However, it is also important to acknowledge that which is "Marxist" about Analytical Marxism. First, "the work of Analytical Marxists self-consciously works on Marxism as a theoretical tradition" (Wright, 1994, p. 191). In other words, they claim the fundamental concerns, themes and arguments of Marxism, and reconstruct them under the "analytical" premises. Second, their empirical questions and theoretical agenda are firmly based on Marxist debates. Third, their conceptual framework is embedded in the Marxist discourse (class, ideology, exploitation, etc.). Finally, Analytical Marxists "share the core normative orientation of Marxism in general" (Ibid, p. 192), that is, a project of emancipation that goes beyond the theoretical agenda.

Accordingly, Wright's work on social class, situated within this school of thought, fully reproduced both its "analytical" and "Marxist" elements. At the same time, as mentioned before, he fully embraced a Marxist political and theoretical position, since "the questions that are at the heart of Marxism continue to be critical for any plausible political project for radical social change" and "the conceptual framework for tackling those questions continues to produce new and insightful answers". However, aware of the reproaches and criticisms that social sciences have posed to Marxism, Wright disagreed with Marxist intellectuals that opted to "dismiss the attacks of non-Marxist social scientists as reflecting bourgeois ideology and/or a positivist methodology" (Wright, 1979, p. 9). He chose to develop instead "empirical research agendas firmly rooted within not only the categories, but the logic, of Marxist theory" (Wright, 1979, p. 10), which pay attention to the theoretical dimensions of variability in "actually existing capitalisms" (Wright, 1985, p. 15)[10].

The discussion of the theoretical context in which Wright's work is situated allows for a better understanding of some elements of his work on class analysis that might seem controversial, such as

---

[10] Thus, Wright rejects the positivist premise that "theory construction is simply a process of empirical generalization of law-like regularities", insisting instead that Marxist theory "should generate propositions about the real world which can be empirically studied" (Wright, 1979, p. 10).

his preoccupation with methodological concerns rather than philosophical ones, or his use of models and quantitative methods to test his hypotheses.

The concept of social class

I will explore Wright's concept of social class by focusing on the chief works in which he developed his own approach to class analysis and his original theory on social classes. The first text is *Class, Crisis and the State* (1978), which contains Wright's first elucidation of his novel approach to class analysis, developed when trying to understand different aspects of the "historically specific contradictions of advance monopoly capitalism" together with the possibilities and constraints for emancipatory movements. The second text, called simply *Classes* (1985), is a study in which our author presented a renewed effort to systematize his concept and theory on class. This study was built from a critical revision of his previous work. In it, Wright modified and expanded upon some of the principles that he established in his first approach. Some of that novel "intellectual direction" was a consequence of his involvement with a new "reference group" of leftist scholars: Analytical Marxists.

Let us start with Wright's goal in formulating a new theory of social class. Our author's careful revision of the different theories and approaches to class analysis resulted in a general diagnosis of the Marxist tradition and a particular diagnosis of the concept of social class. Regarding the first, Wright concluded that there was a lack of strategies within the Marxist tradition that linked research and theory, as well as strategies that connected the analysis of structural processes with empirically observable phenomena. Regarding the second, our author claimed that Marxism had not provided scholars with adequate tools to perform concrete analyses of the contemporary class structure, particularly on what has been colloquially understood as "the middle class"[11]. Wright argued that

---

[11] Wright identifies four types of solutions to the "middle class" problem, all given within the Marxist tradition. First, the "simple polarization" solution, which argues that those social positions which do not "fall" into the working class nor the capitalist class really do belong to the working class, and the lack of polarization is simply a problem of "appearance" or appreciation. Second, the "new

Marx's prediction regarding a growing polarization between classes can't really be taken for granted, and thus, given "the growth of professional and technical occupations and the expansion of managerial hierarchies in large corporations and the state" (Wright, 1985, p. 8), the Marxist tradition needs to take the problem of the diversification of the "wage-earners" seriously. According to Wright, the problem is not so much about the lines of demarcation of the middle class, but "a general theoretical problem of how to conceptualize class relations in capitalist society" (Ibid, p. 26). His goal will then be to "elaborate a comprehensive framework for analyzing class structures in general and for reconceptualizing the problem of the middle class in particular" (Ibid, p. 73).

Let us now analyze some of the arguments presented in *Class, Crisis and the State* (1979). Wright devotes one chapter to the analysis of each one of the concepts that make up the title of the book, which means that there is a chapter dedicated to the "class structure of advanced capitalist societies". The first part of the chapter is dedicated to a review, assessment and critique of Poulantzas' work, considered by Wright as the "the most systematic and thorough attempt to understand precisely the Marxist criteria for classes in capitalist societies" (Wright, 1979, p. 31). While this review will not be explored here, it is important to highlight that Poulantzas was a fundamental influence in Wright's theoretical work[12].

---

petty bourgeoisie" solution, which adopts the concept of "petty bourgeoisie" based on the category of "unproductive labor" or wage-labor which does not produce surplus value (such as professionals or managers). Third, the "new class" solution, which, as it name implies, is the claim that the non-proletarian and non-bourgeoisie positions constitute a historically new class in its own right. This new class has been defined in many different ways; for instance, Gouldner's definition is based on the control of cultural capital, while John Ehrenreich called it "professional-managerial class". Finally, the "middle strata" solution — which according to Wright is either agnostic or avoidant–, which argues that the social positions "caught in-between" the bourgeoisie-proletarian polarization are outside the basic class relation and thus, they are not really "in" any class.

[12] Poulantzas was also concerned with those classes present in "historically determined social formations" that were neither the bourgeoisie nor the proletariat. He called them "autonomous factions of classes" and "distinct classes", and thought they could become "social forces" in specific circumstances.

Wright goes on to present his alternative conceptualization of the contemporary class structure, focusing specifically on those "ambiguous" positions in the class structure, in other words, those positions that are not fully part of the working-class nor the bourgeoisie. According to our author, an analysis of the relations of production in capitalism at the highest level of abstraction reveals two clearly defined, antagonistic and polarized class positions: the workers and the capitalists[13]. However, at more concrete levels of analysis, the study of social formations that articulate and combine the characteristics of different "pure" modes of production reveals other class positions.

For instance, following Poulantzas, Wright identified "simple commodity production" as a non-capitalist mode of production that has always existed in concrete capitalist "social formations". Here, the "petty bourgeoisie" emerges as a class characterized by "having economic ownership and possession of the means of production, but no control over labor power" (Wright, 1979, p. 74). Wright further recognized a series of structural changes in the relations of production of advanced capitalism that have impacted the social processes underlying class relations: "the progressive loss of control over the labor process on the part of the direct producers; the elaboration of complex authority hierarchies within capitalist

---

Poulantzas' theorizations around these ideas, and their application to empirical studies of the petty bourgeoisie, can be considered his main influence on Wright's work.

[13] Later in the book, Wright offers a an "extended definition" of these polar class positions. "The working class can be defined as those positions which: (a) occupy the working class position within the social relations of production, i.e., wage-labor which is excluded from control over money capital, physical capital and labor power; or (b) are linked directly to the working class through immediate family or class trajectories; or (c) occupy working class positions within political or ideological apparatuses, i.e., positions which are excluded from either the creation or execution of state policy and ideology. In a complementary manner, the bourgeois class can be defined as those positions which: (a) occupy the bourgeois position within the social relations of production, i.e., positions of control over money capital, physical capital and labor power; or, (b) are linking directly to the bourgeoisie through families or class trajectories; or (c) occupy bourgeois positions within the political and ideological apparatuses, i.e., positions which involve the control over the creation of state policy and the production of ideology" (Wright, 1979, p. 97).

enterprises and bureaucracies; and the differentiation of various functions originally embodied in the entrepreneurial capitalist" (Ibid, p. 64). The consequence of these changes is the emergence of ambiguous locations in concrete analyses of class relations, which Wright called *contradictory locations within class relations*.

I will introduce here a brief note that will not come up until his next work, but that clarifies Wright's terminology. With this concept, Wright is not talking about the relationship between different classes, which is of course contradictory in itself (in other words, the antagonistic relationship between classes). Instead, the "contradictory locations" are contradictory "in the sense that they partake of both sides of inherently contradictory [class] interests" (Wright, 1985, p. 43), in other words, they are locations that partake in set of class interests that are inherently antagonistic as a result of social relations in capitalism.

There are three "contradictory locations" identified by Wright in *Class, Crisis and the State*: (1) between the proletariat and the bourgeoisie, which includes top managers (who lie in the boundary with the bourgeoisie), middle managers and technocrats, foremen and line supervisors (who lie in the boundary with the working class); (2) between the bourgeoisie and the petty bourgeoisie, such as small employers; (3) between the working class and the petty bourgeoisie, such as certain categories of semi-autonomous workers and others who retain relatively high levels of control over their immediate labor process and conditions. Wright was not happy to leave these categories as theoretical constructs, so he carefully operationalized each one of them using criteria that included economic, social and judicial processes underlying class relations. He even used this operationalization to estimate the distribution of the economically active population of the United States in the three "known classes" and the three "contradictory locations" that he conceived (Wright, 1979, p. 74–87). We thus have a "map" of class structure in advanced capitalism (*Figure 1*).

Figure 1. The relationship of contradictory class positions to class forces in capitalist society

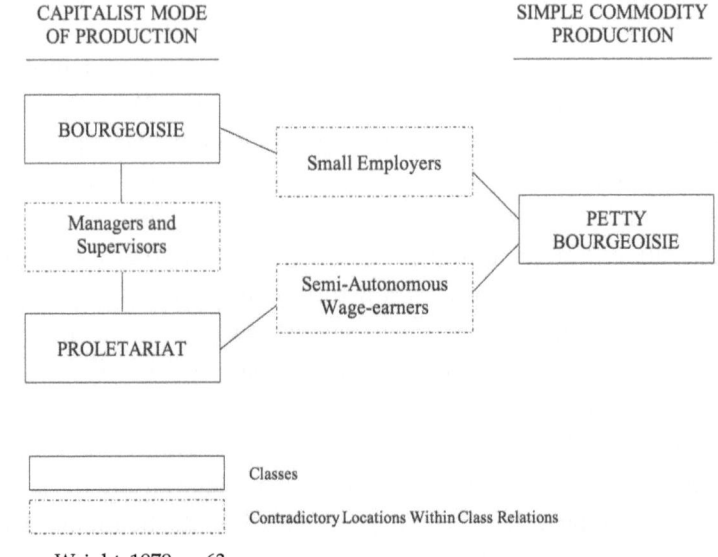

Source: Wright, 1979, p. 63

Finally, Wright acknowledged that there are some positions in the social structure that are not directly determined by the social relations of production, such as that of housewives, students, pensioners, unemployed and welfare recipients, and people employed by the administrative, repressive and ideological apparatus of the state. The class location of these positions, according to our author, is defined by their relationship to the "class interests" (defined in turn within the social relations of production).

Let us now move to Wright's second work, *Classes* (1985). In this text, Wright re-conceptualized the idea of "contradictory locations within class relations" and presented new arguments that wrapped up and polished off his theory on social classes. Additionally, in the second part of the book, "Empirical Investigations", Wright tested his conceptualization of class structure in empirical comparative research through the operationalization of his concepts and categories.

I will begin with Wright's discussion on the distinction between class structure, class formation, class struggle and class consciousness; an analytical distinction that, he argued, does not imply that they exist independently of each other[14]. Class structure refers to "the structure of social relations into which individuals (or in some cases families) enter which determine their class interests" (1985, p. 9). In other words, class structure refers to the "empty spaces" or the "positions" in the structure that are occupied by individuals, rather than the specific individuals that occupy those positions. On the other hand, "class formation" refers to "the formation of organized collectivities within that class structure on the basis of the interests shaped by that class structure" (Ibid, p. 10). In less-abstract terms, Wright refers with this concept to the alliances within and between classes that are formed in specific circumstances. In other words, he refers to the historically developed expressions of class-based collectivities (what some authors would call class-for-itself). By "class struggle" he understands "the forms of conflict engaged in by individuals as class members or by class organizations" (Ibid, p. 28). Finally, "class consciousness" refers to the "class ideologies held by individuals or organizations" (Ibid, p. 28).

Regarding the relationship between these four, which is a fiercely debated issue in the Marxist tradition, Wright argued that the class structure "imposes limits" on class formation, class struggle and class consciousness. In other words and using Marxist language, we could say that class structure determines class formation, class struggle and class consciousness "in the last instance", since it is the class structure which "distributes access to resources in a society, and thus distributes capacities to act" (1985, p. 28). This is not equivalent to saying that there is a simple relation of determination; according to Wright, there are many other elements that play a role in these relationships *within the limits established by the class structure*, including race, gender, ethnicity, legal institutions, etc. The most

---

[14] Wright had introduced a similar discussion in his book *Classes, Crisis and the State*, but it seemed to me that the argumentation put forth in Classes was clearer.

important relationship between these different elements is the one between class structure and class formation—what we would call 'class-in-itself' and 'class-for-itself' in classical Marxist terms. Regarding this relationship, Wright argues that there is a "relative indeterminacy" between these two levels of class analysis (Ibid, p. 123), since the complex mechanisms that operate in differentiated ways within the class structure produce particular collective agents with ideologies and strategies specific to the concrete-historical characteristics of given societies.

As Wright puts it, class structure is the "material basis for a variety of *potential* class formations" (1985, p. 124). Wright did not agree with the assumption that the class structure (class-in-itself) determines a class formation (class-for-itself) on the basis of a "one-to-one relationship", rather, it determines the "underlying probabilities of different kinds of class formation" which may or may not occur in particular-historical circumstances and according to an endless number of factors which are in turn "structurally contingent to class structure itself" (Ibid). In this way, Wright conceded to a structural foundation for class formation, while he also claimed that "it is only through the specific historical analysis of given societies that it is possible to explain what kind of actual formation is built upon that foundation" (Ibid, p. 124). At the other end of this relationship we find what Wright considered the "basic transformative principle" of these analytical relations: class struggle. In other words, class structures, class formations and class consciousness are all transformed by class struggle; this, however, is a transformation that can only be understood as "structurally constrained" (Ibid, p. 30).

Let us briefly look into Wright's arguments regarding structural determination. In order to better understand "structural causality" in Marxist theory, our author elaborated a heuristic "model of determination" that included six distinct kinds of relationships or interconnectedness (six distinct "modes of determination") between different structural categories: selection, mediation, reproduction/nonreproduction, limits of functional compatibility, structural limitation and transformation. These last two are key to the understanding of Wright's interpretation of the dialectical character of determination, that is, the structural constraints and the dynamic movements that occur in any given society. Wright defined *structural limitation* as "a pattern of determination in which a social structure establishes limits within which some other structures or processes can vary, and establishes probabilities for the specific structures or processes that are possible within those limits" (Wright, 1979, p. 16). According to Wright, this mode of determination explains the relationship between the economic structure and the political and ideological superstructure: "economic structures set limits on the possible forms of political and ideological structures, and make some of those possible forms more likely than others, but they do not rigidly determine, in a mechanistic manner, any given form of political or ideological relations" (Ibid). *Transformation* lies at the other end of the heuristic model, which is understood as the "mode of determination by which class struggle (practices) directly affect the processes of structural limitation" (Ibid).

In Wright's model:

> "class struggle, which is itself structurally limited and selected by various social structures, simultaneously reshapes those structures. The word 'simultaneously' is important in this formulation: social structures do not first structurally limit and select class struggle, after which class struggle transforms those structures. Class struggle is intrinsically a process of transformation of structures, and thus the very process which sets limits on class struggle is at the same time transformed by the struggles so limited" (Wright, 1979, p. 21).

Having reviewed Wright's arguments regarding "structural causality", we can move forward to the conceptualization of social class developed in his 1985 work. Our author began by establishing what he considered are the "basic structural properties" of the Marxist concept of social class (1985, p. 34). These properties are:

1. *The concept of class is a relational concept.* This means that social classes can only be defined in terms of their relation with other classes. This is directly contrasted with gradational concepts of class based on quantitative criteria, such as income or education, producing thus a concept in which classes (upper, middle, lower) are not defined by their

relation to each other, but by their relation to the quantitative criteria that delineates them.

2. *The social relations which define classes are intrinsically antagonistic rather than symmetrical.* This principle refers to the fact that classes have intrinsically antagonistic (opposing) interests based on the social relations that define them. As Wright mentioned, the realization of the interests of one class inherently implies the struggle against the realization of the interests of the other class. This principle will serve the basis of Wright's idea regarding "contradictory class locations". As mentioned before, they are contradictory in the sense that individuals in these locations partake of a set of class interests that are, by definition, opposing.

3. *The objective basis of this antagonistic interests is exploitation.* Wright highlights this property in order to differentiate his concept of class from those that are defined on the basis of relations of domination or oppression. I will expand upon this difference later in the text.

4. *The fundamental basis of exploitation is to be found in the social relations of production.* With this principle, Wright reminds us that class is firmly anchored in the relations of production.

These four principles, along with the ones established in his discussion of distinct "modes of determination", comprise the conceptual framework used by Wright to "transform the ideological concept of 'middle class' into a theoretical concept" (Wright, 1985, p. 37). He began by acknowledging some problems with the concept of "contradictory locations within class relations" developed in *Classes, Crisis and the State*. Some of them, he argued, are relatively minor, such as his categorization of "semi-autonomous employees"[15]. There is one, however, which is "the most fundamental": the fact that his concept rested on relations of *domination*, rather than *exploitation*

---

[15] Wright acknowledged three problems with his arguments around semi-autonomous employees: "the claim that autonomy is a petty-bourgeois property of class relations; the relatively unstable or undetermined character of autonomy in certain work settings; and empirical anomalies in the use of the concept" (Wright, 1985, p. 53).

(like most neo-Marxist approaches to class structure). This modification, that is, going from a concept built upon relations of exploitation rather than domination, will be the cornerstone of the new conceptualization of "contradictory locations within class relations".

Let us briefly examine this transition. According to Wright, the concept of domination is not anchored to the relations of production, and thus to the relations of exploitation that are their consequence. Therefore, domination does not imply inherently opposing material interests (Wright, 1985, p. 56). For instance, there is a relation of domination in a parent-child relationship, but it does not imply the existence of antagonistic interests nor is there a reference to exploitation in the social relations of production. Additionally, a concept centered on domination can easily lead to "multiple oppression" approaches to understanding society, that is, interpretations in which social relations are characterized by different forms of domination (race, ethnicity, gender, socioeconomic status, nationality). In these approaches, there is no theoretical possibility that allows for one of these multiple oppressions to have an explanatory priority over any other one[16].

Wright's use of the concept of exploitation is based on John Roemer's work[17]. The main idea underlying this notion of exploitation is that "one person's welfare is obtained at the expense of the other" (Wright, 1985, p. 65), which is an antagonistic relation that is well acknowledge by the Marxist tradition — the income and wealth of one class comes from the appropriation of the surplus labor performed by another class. "The rich are rich *because* the poor are poor" (Ibid). Exploitation has thus a distinct character which makes reference to both (a) the objective antagonism of material class

---

[16] Wright established a distinction between "economic exploitation" and "economic oppression", where exploitation "includes both economic oppression and the appropriation of the fruits of labor of one class by another" (Wright, 1985, p. 74).

[17] Our author invoked, for the most part, Roemer's arguments from *A General Theory of Exploitation and Class* (1982).

interests and (b) the interdependency of opposing classes[18]. There is another implication to the use of Roemer's concept of exploitation, which is that "the material basis of exploitation lies in inequalities in the distribution of productive assets, usually referred to as property relations" (Wright, 1985, p. 72). According to Wright, exploitation based on the "property of productive assets" is close tied to the classical Marxist notion of exploitation based on the "property of the means (assets) of production". Wright's identification of a connection between exploitation and the property of assets evolved into a claim that there are different mechanisms for exploitation based on the property of different assets.

According to our author, there two types of assets whose property generate exploitation: organization assets and qualification assets. The first ones are defined as "the conditions of coordinated cooperation among producers in a complex division of labor" (Wright, 1985, p. 79) and its property — or lack of it — is reflected in forms of authority and hierarchy. In advanced capitalist societies, they are controlled by managers and capitalists. On the other hand, qualification assets refer to the "property of credentials which have the effect of restricting the supply of skills" (Ibid, p. 76). In other words, these are assets that can only be obtained through highly restrictive mechanisms that confer credentials which, in turn, produce and reproduce skill differentials[19].

These new formulations and arguments regarding different dimensions of relations of exploitation provided Wright with the conceptual tools to analyze social classes in contemporary capitalism, particularly as they related to the middle or indeterminate classes. Accordingly, there are two types of "non-polarized contradictory locations". First, there are class locations that are "neither

---

[18] Based on his review and dialogue with Roemer's work, Wright's defined exploitation as "an economically oppressive appropriation of the fruits of the labor of one class by another" (Wright, 1985, p. 77).

[19] Wright briefly mentioned some examples of these mechanisms: "restrictions on the numbers of people admitted to the schools which confer credentials; cultural criteria may be established for admission to schools; the immediate costs of obtaining a credential may be prohibitively high, etc." (Wright, 1985, p. 101).

exploiters nor exploited" (Ibid, p. 86); people in these locations have a proportional property of the asset in question, for instance, a self-employed person who is neither exploited nor exploiter within the relations of production. Second, "positions that are exploiting along one dimension of exploitation relations, while on another are exploited" (Ibid, p. 87), such as high-skilled wage-earners, who are exploited in terms of ownership of productive assets, but exploiters in terms of ownership of qualification assets. Wright argues that such a pattern of "intersecting exploitation relations" is only possible because concrete-historical societies are not characterized by one single mode of production, and neither are their resulting class structures.

Accordingly, we have a second "map" or typology of class structure (*Figure 2*) that takes into account the complexity of class locations in contemporary capitalist societies, which are different from the polarized classes in the capitalist mode of production (bourgeoisie and proletariat). There are two elements that must be taken into consideration when looking at this new typology. First, the principal relation of exploitation is the one that divides the owners from the non-owners of the means of production (as is shown in the two-segment division). Second, these are still "contradictory locations within class—and exploitation—relations" because the interests of all the intermediate classes will be contradictory concerning the primary form of class struggle in capitalism—the struggle between labor and capital. Thus, "on the one hand, [the middle classes] are like workers in being excluded from ownership of the means of production; on the other, they have interests opposed to workers because of their effective control of organization and skill assets" (Wright, 1985, p. 8).

Figure 2. Wright's typology of class locations in capitalist society

	Owners of means of production	Non-owners [wage-earners]		
Own sufficient capital to hire workers and not work	1. Bourgeoisie	4. Expert managers	7. Semi-credentialled managers	10. Uncredentialled managers
Own sufficient capital to hire workers but must work	2. Small employers	5. Expert supervisors	8. Semi-credentialled supervisors	11. Uncredentialled supervisors
Own sufficient capital to work for sell but not to hire workers	3. Petty bourgeoisie	6. Expert non-managers	9. Semi-credentialled workers	12. Proletarians
		+ Qualification assets −		
			+ Organization assets −	

Source: Wright, 1985, p. 88

This conceptualization of social class is not static. Instead, it recognizes that "the principle forms of contradictory locations will vary historically depending on the particular combination of exploitation relations in a given society" (Wright, 1985, p. 89). This leads to a fundamental distinction between, on the one hand, Wright's *theory*, which is built upon the acknowledgment of the different relations of exploitation generated by the property of different assets (productive, organization and qualification assets) and, on the other hand, its *concrete application* (i.e. the typology presented in *Figure 2*) which identifies specific classes and class-locations in concrete-historical societies, including contemporary capitalism.

Finally, Wright claimed that all class systems are supported by processes that legitimize them. In other words, he argued that the stable reproduction of class systems required some sort of consensus regarding the legitimacy of the class structure. Our author identified two ideologies that confer this legitimacy and defend privilege: one which appeals to "rights" and another that appeals to "the general welfare". Examples of rights to defend privilege go from those that appealed to divine or blood mandates to justify classes (as it was done in feudalism), to the appeal of the "natural right" of people to the fruits of their property (as it is done in capitalism). The "general welfare" arguments are, according to Wright, more durable and pervasive. He defined them as the "defenses of a system of inequality — in our terms a class system — which claim that the underprivileged would in fact be worse off in the absence of the greater benefits enjoyed by the privileged" (Ibid, p. 119). For instance, the idea that workers would do worse if capitalists did not risk and invest the surplus value they obtain. These ideologies are further supported by an objective motivational basis, which is related to Göran Therborn's ideas on the motivational requirements of capitalism and their antagonism with the motivations of actors (Therborn, 1980). In Wright's words, "capitalism engenders the kinds of motivations that are necessary to make capitalism work" (Wright, 1985, p. 121).

There is a final comment that I would like to add here regarding Wright's arguments on "class compromise" developed in his final work, *Understanding Class* (2015). Our author recuperated

Gramsci's ideas on the hegemony of the dominant class (where class relations are sustained by a combination of coercion and consensus) to argue that it is possible for "opposing" classes to reach a positive "compromise", where no part entirely loses or wins. In other words, Wright claimed that there is a possibility for the popular power of the working class and the interests of the capitalist class—two instances that traditionally are regarded as antagonistic—to reach an equilibrium. There are three different institutional spheres where these compromises can take place: political relations, market relations, and productive relations. Thus, this premise sheds light on the emergence of different forms of working-class collective organization (from unions to political parties), concessions that are achieved through the regulation of capital (welfare systems or worker rights), or Keynesian-type social pacts.

Wright's concept of class: implications and significance

> "Not only have there been a hundred years of theoretical discussions of the problem of class since Marx's death, there have also been a hundred years of history, and if Marxist theory is at all scientific one would expect conceptual advances to have occurred in such a period."
> Erik Olin Wright[20]

Wright's work could be considered as the most sophisticated and rigorous analysis of the class structure in contemporary capitalism. His initial concern over the Marxist treatment of middle classes evolved into a theory that re-established some of the classical elements of Marxism (the centrality of exploitation, the inherent antagonism between classes, the rootedness of class to the social relations of production) and re-connected them to new and innovative constructs that bring the classical formulation of class closer to its contemporary reality. The notion of "contradictory locations within class relations" allows for the understanding of the relationship between classes that are indeed in an "intermediate" or "in-between" location in the polarization between the bourgeoisie and proletariat,

---

[20] *Classes* (Wright, 1985, p. 16).

but that have a much more problematic existence: they partake in contradictory interests, they occupy complex locations in the class structure, they have qualitatively different relationships with each one of the polarized classes, etc.

Additionally, Wright's work took on one of Marxism's greatest challenges: bridging the distance between abstract theories and empirical analysis. The American sociologist elaborated a middle-range theory that engaged both with the careful construction of a coherent and consistent conceptual apparatus and the operationalization of each one of those conceptual formulations. I did not go over Wright's "empirical investigations" in this revision of his work, such as the comparative analysis of the class structures of the United States and Sweden developed in *Classes* (1985). However, I must note that he dedicated broad and detailed sections of his books and articles to empirical quantitative analyses of the class structure in contemporary capitalism. These analyses are securely rooted in the precepts that he considered as non-negotiable principles of any Marxist approach to the study of class.

Finally, Wright's concept of class begets an important political implication. The recognition that there are no simple polarized class structures in "actually existing capitalisms" opens the door to different possibilities for transformation; a transformation that includes compromises with "contradictory locations within class relations" built through political mediations (Wright, 1985, p. 286–290). As Wright himself says, "one of the consequences of this reconceptualization of the middle class is that it is no longer axiomatic that the proletariat is the unique, or perhaps even universally central, rival to the capitalist class power in capitalist society" (Wright, 1985, p. 89).

Let's end by mentioning briefly some of the main problems in the work of the American sociologist. First, while his exchanges with other theoretical traditions and theorists allows for a less rigid conceptual apparatus, Wright's excessive theoretical pluralism can also be problematic. Rose and Marshall (1989) argue that Wright's theory blurs the distinction between a neo-Weberian and a neo-Marxist analysis of class structure. Indeed, Weber (1946) gave a central role to credentials and other assets (skills, property, services, organizational position) in the determination of "life chances" and, in turn, "market situations", that define what he understood as a social class. While I will not expand upon what might seem like Weberian and neo-Weberian elements in Wright's theory, it is true that the central role given to concepts such as "organization assets", "qualification assets" and "credentials"–concepts which were widely used by scholars that study social mobility, inequality and stratification—seems to downplay his claim of emphasizing a Marxist perspective of exploitation and conflict.

A second key criticism has to do with the absence of an analysis of class as "collectivities" (Rose & Marshall, 1989, p. 261). While Wright does consider "class formation" as a key element of class analysis, he does not explain the process by which it takes place; his focus lies solely on the explanation of its relation to class structure. It could be said that, by directing all his attention to the definition of class structure, he leaves a relative theoretical gap regarding class action and its trajectory to collective action.

Despite these shortcomings, Erik Olin Wright's theory of class cannot but stand out for its courageous conceptual innovation. The questions that it raised and the debates that it fostered have greatly enriched the Marxist tradition, and we can anticipate that they will do so for a very long time.

References

Elster, J. (1982). Marxism, functionalism and game theory. *Theory and Society* 11: 453–482.

Elster, J. (1985). *Making sense of Marx*. Cambridge University Press.

Roemer, J. (1982). *A General Theory of Exploitation and Class*. Harvard University Press.

Therborn, G. (1980). *The Power of Ideology and the Ideology of Power*. Verso.

Weber, M. (1946). Class, Status and Party. In *From Max Weber: Essays in Sociology*. Oxford University Press.

Wright, E. O. (1979). *Classes, Crisis and the State*. Verso

Wright, E. O. (1980). "Varieties on Marxist conceptions on class structure". *Politics and Society*. Vol. 9: 323–370

Wright, E. O. (1985). *Classes*. Verso.

Wright, E. O. (1989). Rethinking, once again, the concept of class structure. In E. O. Wright. *The debate on classes*. Verso.

Wright, E. O. (1994). *Interrogating Inequality: essays on class analysis, socialism and Marxism*. Verso.

Wright, E. O. (2005). Class. In G. Ritzer (Ed). *Encyclopedia of Social Theory*. Sage Publications.

Wright, E. O. (2015). *Understanding class*. Verso.

Chapter 6

From mass-worker to multitude: the metamorphosis of the class subject in Italian *operaismo* and post-*operaismo*

Massimo Modonesi and Matari Pierre Manigat

In this chapter, we will give an account of the contributions of Italian *operaismo* (workerism) and post-*operaismo* to the debate on social class. We will focus on the arguments found in the work of Mario Tronti and Antonio Negri, and the latter in particular, since it is an author whose production has extended and amplified to the present.

The main contributions of this school of thought derive from the study of the different forms adopted by social labor in contemporary capitalism: mass-worker, social-worker and multitude are three categories that demarcate the limits of the compositions and recompositions of the class subject. In the classical way of Marxism, the *operaistas* and post-*operaistas* conduct their analyses in two simultaneous spheres: the socioeconomic one and the sociopolitical one. While the first one considers the implications of the generalization of certain forms of production (going from Taylorism-Fordism to post-Fordism), the second examines the organic political form of these forms of production. Thus, the transit from the Planner-State to the Empire constitutes the correlate of the transit of the worker-mass to the multitude.

The conceptual sequence worker-mass, social worker, multitude not only mirrors three historical states of the class of producers, but highlights continuities and ruptures within the *operaista* tradition. This is also reflected in the way we present our arguments in this chapter. We first examine the genealogy of the concept of mass-worker. Next, we show how, as of the late 1970s, the notion of social worker foreshadowed methodological concerns and theoretical changes that responded to the challenge of defining the class subject under globalization. We end with a reflection on the elaboration of the concept of multitude, parent and antagonistic correlate to the Empire.

The worker-mass and class composition

Operaismo was the most innovative political and intellectual movement that came out of the struggles that characterized the social history of Italy during the 1960s and until the end of the 1970s[1]. *Operaismo* stood out for the approach proposed by Raniero Panzieri, translator of the second volume of *Capital* and founder of the *Quaderni Rossi* in 1961, the first *operaista* journal. Panzieri understood Marxism as a "union of sociology, economy and politics"[2]. He dissected Marx's work and distinguished between a "dead Marxism" and a "living Marxism". While the first one forgoes the intervention of the subjectivity of the producers, the second one apprehends the dynamic of capitalism in the intersection of class struggle and productive forces. Marx's analysis of the character of the big factory and its dynamics — the dialectic between workers' struggles and the introduction and perfection of machines — is the illustration of living Marxism par excellence[3]. This interpretation of the relationship between technology and social struggle catapulted a field of "research on the working class" — its condition, its power and its role in the process of capital accumulation — taken up by different *operaista* thinkers in the beginning of the 1960s[4]. According to Mario Tronti, one of the intellectual icons of *operaismo*:

---

[1] For a history of Italian Marxism and the place and role of *operaismo* in it, see the pioneer synthesis by Cristina Corradi, "Storia del marxismo in Italia" (2005).

[2] See the anthology of Raniero Panzieri's work "La ripresa del marxismo-leninismo in Italia" (1977) and the essay by Ferraris "Raniero Panzieri: per un socialism della democrazia diretta" (2011).

[3] Panzieri claimed that Marx's 1859 preface to *A Contribution to the Critique of Political Economy* was the origin and quintessence of "dead Marxism" (Potier, 1986, p. 407–408).

[4] The qualifier *"operaismo"* was originally adopted by Panzieri's adversaries in order to denounce his conceptualization of the relationship between the economic and the political elements. See Potier (1986, p. 401–404) and Bologna (2011).

> "After Marx, no one has known anything new about the working class. It still remains an unknown continent. We know that it exists, of course, because we've all heard it being talked about, and anyone can read all manner of fabulous tales about it. But no one can say: I saw, I understood" (Tronti, 2019, p. 45).

The concept of social worker emerged from the studies on the working class headed by Panzieri's methodological contributions regarding the juncture between the socioeconomic and the sociopolitical structures, in other words, between the infrastructure and the superstructure.

There are two concepts that advance the analyses of the infrastructure and superstructure in this first stage of *operaismo*, which was marked by the height of Fordism and Keynesianism: the social factory and the planner-State. The social factory designates the reality that stems from the emergence of the *company towns*, the entanglement between workers' factories, cities and neighborhoods during the industrialization of the north of Italy, a territory that was privileged by the studies and the actions of the *operaista* militant groups (Tronti, 1962). This extension of the logic of the social factory to broader society is mediated by the existence of a specific state form that Negri defined as a planner-State; a sort of "collective capitalist" that, under the appearance of mediating between capital and labor, organizes exploitation at a social scale and guarantees the discipline of Fordist work.

The emergence and the reproduction of the mass-worker are both the result of the consolidation of the social factory, as well as the actions of the planner-State. The mass-worker refers, objectively and subjectively, to the mutation of what the *operaistas* called *class composition*. Inspired by Marx's concept of "organic composition of capital", the concept of class composition was introduced to avoid the petrification of the notion of class and capture instead its changing configuration. The technical composition of the working class refers to the technological conditions of production as well the division of labor and its forms of organization. Its political composition, on the other hand, refers to the class subjectivity, that is, the externalization of the elements that integrate the history of the political struggles and organizations of class, based on the behaviors, needs, desires and cultures of the workers. In this way, the mass-worker simultaneously adopts the characteristics of the direct producer considered in the postwar industrial conditions and its character of a tendentially insubordinate subject.

The study of class composition thus became an object of interest for the *operaista* authors and militants during the 1960s and 70s. Objectively, they identified the rise of the centrality of the professional worker — workers that would have a certain scope for intervention in the productive process given their possession of certain technical knowledge and abilities — with the emergence of the mass-worker, the non-qualified worker, a mere cog in the Fordist assembly line.

This diagnosis was confirmed by the characteristics of the workers' struggles that took place in the beginning of the 60s and that spread in the following years; radical and spontaneous struggles led by young workers, for the most part migrants from Southern Italy, recently hired, weakly integrated to unions, and placed in the lowest strata of the labor hierarchy. These workers were part of a generation whose studies and expectations distanced them from their parents, but who ended up as wage-laborers just like them, growing and feeding frustrations and rejection towards the current standards of social integration. These struggles were opposed to the conciliatory attitude of the unions, and instead outlined a radical rejection of the despotism in the factory. The *operaistas* saw here an anticapitalist potential, which explains their concerns and efforts to understand every detail of the new conditions that shaped the new class subject. The subversive and antagonistic character of this "new" worker stood out and refreshed the revolutionary hypotheses. These efforts were captured in a methodological approach called *conricerca* — a model and practice of participatory research outlined and applied, for the most part, by Romano Alquati. This approach implied a relationship and close collaboration between researchers and workers, which would allow for a thorough knowledge of the experience of class and promote, at the same time, the latter's acquisition of consciousness[5].

---

[5] See the dossier "Uso socialista della inchiesta operaia" (Panzieri, 1965, p. 67-269).

But the main contribution and theoretical provocation of *operaism* – its Copernican revolution, as it was called – is the methodological inversion of the traditionally accepted relation between capital accumulation and class struggle formulated by Tronti in the 60s:

> "We too saw capitalist development first and the workers second. This is a mistake. Now we have to turn the problem on its head, change orientation, and start again from first principles, which means focusing on the struggle of the working class" (Tronti, 2019, p. 184).

Capital thus became the dependent variable, and the development of capitalism was conceptualized as a permanent process of adjustment aimed at holding back the indomitable push of living work. Indeed, the cycles of capital accumulation shape the answers to workers' struggles. It is through them that capital aims to decompose class as a subject and generate a new cycle of class recomposition. This consistent inversion in understanding capital through class struggle, or more exactly, through the construction and the initiative of the antagonistic class (the working class), led to innovative theoretical and political perspectives.

If the movements of the working class are historically and logically prior to capital, then the laws of the development of capital are, deep down, "laws of the capitalist development of the working class". While Tronti claimed a "Leninist correction of Marx" by putting the theory of revolution ahead of the critique of political economy, he argued that Marx found class inside and against capital, since the working class can only be understood based on its forms of struggle (Tronti, 2019).

In the programmatic landscape, this analytical premise was supportive of a radicalization that was materialized in a new articulation between social struggle and political struggle. For example, the classic matter of wage vindication was no longer considered as a place of negotiation, but as one of irreducible antagonism. This involved fighting for higher wages that were not tied to growth in productivity, so as to break the logic of capital. Similarly, the fight aimed for the implementation of guaranteed salaries and wage egalitarianism in order to end the hierarchies and divisions inside the factory and in society more generally. Going further, workers' fights should transcend the matter of wages and working conditions and extend to the reappropriation of social wealth in terms of use value: housing, transportation, assets, etc. In the last instance, being a worker implied an ulterior rupture in relation to labor; the so-called rejection of work, the rejection of commodification, and a total estrangement of the worker with respect to the means of production that would lead to sabotage, absenteeism and other forms of struggle that aimed to find a political outlet to alienation, given that workers' intelligence should not be dedicated to production but to militancy.

The social worker and class recomposition

Negri came up with the notion of social worker in the 70s with this combination of theoretical and political matters in the background. This notion complements, displaces and eventually substitutes the concept of mass-worker as the preeminent subject that arises from class recomposition and is increasingly placed at the heart of the struggle against capital. This transition reveals a leap in regards to the continuity and rupture of traditional *operaismo* and workers' autonomism, and it will open the door to post-*operaismo* and the emergence of the concept of multitude.

The notion of social worker indicates, first and foremost, the gestation of a new class composition, emphasizing the subjective transformations that accompanied the crisis of Fordism-Keynesianism related to the development of the service sector (or tertiarization) as an extension of wage labor. In 1975 Negri developed ideas on self-valorization, proletarian independence, counterpower, and rejection of work. These ideas highlighted the antagonistic character of an expanded working class, the social worker, which stood out for its subversive and insubordinate profile. Negri's arguments are anchored on the principle of the extension of the social factory, assuming that if all productive labor is wage labor, society is a diffuse factory inhabited by a diffuse type of worker, which can be called social. The working class thus turns into the proletariat in a wide sense: a class that is not only apprehended in the fields of production and capitalist circulation, but in its reproduction as a labor force based on its necessities, consumptions and cultures. Additionally, these are all fields of relative independence and autonomy with respect to capital, and thus allow for an accumulation of force that could externalize as struggle[6].

However, beyond the reaffirmation of the basic principle of *operaismo* — which claims that capital adapts to class struggle, rather than the other way around — and the wide variety of forms of struggle — in particular the emergence of cooperation as a pillar of "self-valorization" rather than a pillar of "rejection to work"–, the use of the notion of social worker was a symptom of the urgency to integrate tendencies that, since the late 70s, signaled the decline of the centrality of the industrial worker as the subject in charge of social work. This led to a reevaluation of the entire enterprise.

Negri had already outlined in 1982 the need to surpass the "old categories" (Negri, 2006, p. 13–174). He thus formally defined the antagonistic subject as a "multiple collective complexity" (Negri, 2006, p. 118), which increased the flexibility of the concept of class based on the "complexity, differences and multiplicity of struggles and antagonistic behaviors that we really observe" (Ibid, p. 21). According to Negri, since the late 70s the "scene of social transformations" bore witness to the proliferation of "new collective subjectivities" that reflected "modifications in the social organization of labor", as well as "transformations of its social qualification". Negri claimed that "the antagonisms borne by those subjectivities cannot be recovered in the traditional horizon of the political" (Negri, 1999a, p. 33–35).

This contraposition between unity and multiplicity tightened the concept of class, which opened the way for an appropriation of the concepts of biopolitics and rhizome from Michel Foucault and Félix Guattari, respectively[7]. These two inclusions promoted a reformulation of the constitution of social relations in general and, above all, blurred the distinctions between the economic, political,

---

[6] These ideas were especially developed in "Proletari e Stato" (1977) and "Il dominio e il sabotaggio" (1979), but they are present in all of Negri's texts from the 70s.
[7] As well as an influence from Spinoza. See Negri (1981).

social and cultural spheres. Furthermore, these inclusions would have two important implications in Negri's definition of the subject in charge of social work in contemporary capitalism: first, a radicalization of the subjective dimension in the notion of class composition, and second, a new perspective in the "production of forms of subjectivities", to overcome what Negri called the "sequential logic" of capitalism (Negri, 1999b, p. 22–24).

This reevaluation of these matters led to changes in the meaning of the flexibilization of the concept of class: the concepts of social worker and working class disappeared; first at the hands of the empty category of subject and then later on, at the hands of the notion of multitude.

Multitude or social cooperation on a global scale

In order to arrive at the concept of multitude, Negri had to reformulate his analyses of capitalist infrastructure and superstructure prevalent since the 80s. Similar to how the concept of mass-worker emerged from the study of Fordism and the planner-State, the analysis of production in the age of globalization, as well as its main political form, catapulted the concept of multitude. However, unlike *operaismo*, post-*operaismo* revolutionized the method of articulation of the economic and political instances. The concept of "Integrated Global Capitalism" (IGC) is the ancestor of what Negri and Hardt would later call "Empire". The Empire is to be found precisely in the process of "de-territorialization" of authority and, its correlate, the impossibility of locating authority, which announce the emergence of a "postnational political and legal form" (Negri, 1999c, p. 37–41).

There are two ways in which we could track the construction of the concept of Empire. First, following a general and abstract approach, we could trace Negri and Hardt's reflections on the State, Law and Sovereignty[8]. From this essay's perspective, we should instead examine the problem following the red thread of the *operaista* interpretation: capital adapts to the social struggles. Negri and

---

[8] This reflection can be traced to the publication of "The constituent power" in 1992 (Negri ,1999e).

Hardt followed this principle and claimed that the genesis of the Empire is parallel to the formation of what they call global society and, later on, multitude (Negri, 1999b, p. 43). In this way, the Empire emerges as a result of the deployment of the subjectivities of the collective labor forces in the 20th century. This process had two great moments: the New Deal and decolonization. While the first one "produced the highest form of disciplinary government", the second one opened the door to the expiration of the nation-State.

The twilight of the nation-State as a political form, invokes two structuring processes of the contemporary global economy: the universalization of wage-labor as a form of social existence of the workforce, and the full realization of the global market. The need to organize the global market is precisely what justifies the emergence of a post-national political form:

> "At this point the capitalist regimes have to undergo a process of reform and restructuring in order to ensure their capacity to organize the world market. This tendency emerges clearly only in the 1980s (and is established definitively after the collapse of the Soviet model of modernization), but already at the moment of its first appearance its principal features are clearly defined. It has to be a new mechanism of the general control of the global process and thus a mechanism that can coordinate politically the new dynamics of the global domain of capital and the subjective dimensions of the actors; it has to be able to articulate the imperial dimension of command and the transversal mobility of the subjects" (Hardt & Negri, 2001, p. 254).

But multitude is not only characterized by its contradictory relationship (training/insubordination) to the discipline required by the Empire. Negri's reflections rest upon the redefinition of the concept of production, and thus, of social work.

Negri understands process of production as "the production of useful assets, production of communication and social solidarity, production of aesthetic universes, production of freedom" (Negri, 1999d, p. 69). The definition further indicates that the "center of gravity of these productive processes dislocated", going from the centrality of workers to the "molecular plots of minorities and marginalized people" (Ibid). Here lies the great transformation of social work of the late 20th century; productivity in work is no longer exclusively incumbent upon industry workers, but upon all of the participants of social cooperation. Thus, the profile of the class subject in contemporary capitalism changed to that of a swirl of wage workers and non-wage workers; workers whose only common characteristic is cooperation in the social production. Hardt and Negri formally define the multitude as "all those who work under the rule of capital and thus potentially as the class of those who refuse the rule of capital" (Hardt & Negri, 2004, p. 106). This is the objective difference between the working class that emerged from the industrial revolution and the multitude.

The redefinition of the process of production and the difference between the working class and the multitude ultimately respond to changes in the form and content of social labor in contemporary capitalism. The concept of *immaterial labor* that appeared in Negri's works in the first years of the 1990s goes beyond a mere acknowledgment of the twilight of the centrality of industry. Instead, it proposes a positive definition of the new content of social labor. Thus, the notion of *immaterial labor* highlights the centrality of a worker who is dedicated to "a labor of control, of handling of information, a decision-making capacity that involves the investment of subjectivity" (Lazzarato & Negri, 2001, p. 23). This centrality is accompanied by the development of new productive and cooperation forces that are captured in the Marxian concept of *General Intellect*, which is defined by a double transformation; that of labor into immaterial labor, and that of workforce into "mass intellectuality" (Ibid, p. 25). Under the laws of private property of the means of production, these productive forces lead to a society characterized by the "exploitation of the production and expression of knowledge" (Hardt & Negri, 2012, p. 55).

Immaterial labor entails the production of assets such as knowledge, information, communication or emotional responses. It is a biopolitical labor; a notion that the authors use to avoid reducing labor to wage-labor, and thus include "human creative capacities in all their generality" (Hardt & Negri, 2004, p. 105). The immediate consequence of this definition of immaterial or biopolitical labor is that the experience of exploitation is no longer the only sphere of constitution of workers' subjectivities. Thus, far from disappearing, exploitation is now present in the dimensions of communication and cooperation as the "expropriation of cooperation and the nullification of the meanings of linguistic production" (Hardt & Negri, 2001, p. 385). Hence, the exploitation of immaterial labor, and its corresponding productive processes, characterize the current phase of capitalism: cognitive capitalism.

The multitude designates the class subject that emerges with globalization and the centrality of immaterial labor (Hardt & Negri, 2004). According to Hardt and Negri, the two-dimensional definition of the concept of multitude—socioeconomic and biopolitical—overcomes some of the vices in the traditional definitions of class. In contrast with the liberal tradition, which continuously expands upon the social categories of "economic class" based on differences in income, wealth, race, ethnicity, etc., the Marxist tradition claims that "in capitalist society there tends to be a simplification of class categories such that all forms of labor tend to merge into a single subject, the proletariat, which confronts capital" (Hardt & Negri, 2004, p. 103). Thus, while the first tradition tends to multiply social categories, the second one tends to reduce them. While "both perspectives are, in fact, true", they are also unilateral.

The multitude—or social labor force at a global scale—adopts the shape of a rhizome and is expressed as an "ensemble of productive constellations of subjectivity" (Negri, 2000, p. 403). For Hardt and Negri, the singularities that conform the multitude should not merge their struggles. Rather, they should articulate those singularities around "the common wealth", and form a movement of moments founded in cooperation and struggle, rather than identity. It is thus that, politically, the multitude develops several forms of resistance against the Empire[9] (Hardt & Negri, 2004, p. 63–69). Hardt and Negri utilize this framework to analyze different the social movements that inaugurated a new cycle of struggles since 2011—from Cairo to New York, by way of Athens and Madrid. Despite their differences, these movements shared two important characteristics: first, they came up with distinct forms of horizontal organization that developed genuine types of participation and democratic decision-making. Second, "these were struggles for the

---

[9] See the work of Judith Revel (2008, p. 24–27).

common, in the sense that they contest the injustices of neoliberalism and, ultimately, the rule of private property" (Hardt & Negri, 2012, p. 5).

By way of its own constitution, the multitude opens the way to a series of possible outcomes. Indeed, "the flesh of the multitude consists of a series of conditions that are ambivalent: they could lead toward liberation or be caught in a new regime of exploitation and control" (Hardt & Negri, 2004, p. 212). This dilemma implies a need for a political project of the multitude, for its mobilization around and for "the common". In this way, Negri acknowledges two levels in its formation: the ontological multitude, and the political multitude. The first one is present, the second one dormant. In the second level, he envisions the historical possibility of intensive cycles of struggle (as opposed to extensive, thematic, spatial or global cycles).

Ultimately, the concept of multitude is an innovative attempt to define the doble dimension—objective and subjective—of what Marx called "collective worker" in the concrete social, technological, political and cultural conditions of the present time.

Conclusion

The conceptual sequence mass-worker, social worker and multitude designates the deep transformation of the class subject that took place from the postwar until today, as well as the transition from Fordism to the current globalization regime. Using *operaista* language, we could say that this sequence is the guiding theme in the history of class composition. Despite the differences and discrepancies mentioned above, there is methodological unity in the *operaista* and post-*operaista* reflections. The three concepts speak for particular historical tendencies, real abstractions, specific forms of social antagonism and modes of constitution of subjectivities; four elements that constitute the cardinal points of the Marxist method according to Hardt and Negri (2004).

The great ambition of these authors' trilogy lies in the assessment and criticism of the old interpretative tools, as well as supplying the class subject that emerged with globalization with new conceptual and critical devices. The authors do not hesitate to present their work as the equivalent of what the *Communist Manifesto* was to the 19th century proletariat. The definition of multitude rises up the challenge of creating a category that incorporates two tendencies of social reality: the universalization of the condition of wage-labor—just as Marx anticipated—and the proliferation of a multiplicity of differentiations irreducible to any type of homogenization. This is precisely what the concept of multitude implies when defined as "singularities that act in common" (Hardt & Negri, 2004: 105). In this way, multitude is the class subject that determines and faces the political and legal form that is the Empire.

But the transit of the mass-worker to the multitude not only describes the transformation of the class subject. It highlights ruptures both within the *operaista* tradition and with Marxism more generally, which places post-*operaismo* in the indeterminate galaxy of post-Marxism. Still, the originality, innovation and even the controversy of the theorizations of *operaismo* and post-*operaismo* makes them relevant contributions to the Marxist debate on social classes since the 60s and until today.

Translated by María Vignau Loría

References

Altamira, C. (2006). *Los marxismos del nuevo siglo*. Biblos.

Balestrini, N. & Moroni, P. (1997). *L'orda d'oro 1968–1977*. Feltrinelli.

Bologna, S. (2011). L'operaismo italiano. In P. P. Poggio, *L'altronovecento. Comunismo eretico e pensiero critico (Vol. II)*. Jaca Book.

Cristina, C. (2005). *Storia del marxismo in Italia*. Manifestolibri.

Ferraris, P. (2011). Raniero Panzieri: per un socialismo della democrazia diretta. In P. P. Poggio, *L'altro novecento. Comunismo eretico e pensiero critico (Vol. II)*. Jaca Book.

Hardt, M. & Negri, A. (2001). *Empire*. Harvard University Press

Hardt, M. & Negri, A. (2003). *El trabajo de Dionisos*. Akal.

Hardt, M. & Negri, A. (2004). *Multitude: War and Democracy in the Age of the Empire*. Penguin Press

Hardt, M. & Negri, A. (2009). *Commonwealth*. Harvard University Press.

Hardt, M. & Negri, A. (2012). *Declaration*. New York: Argo-Navis.

Lazzarato, M. & Negri, A. (2001). *Trabajo inmaterial. Formas de vida y producción de subjetividad*. DP&A Editora.

Negri, A. (1977). *Proletari e Stato. Per una discussione su autonomia operaia e compromesso storico*. Feltrinelli.

Negri, A. (1979). *Il dominio e il sabotaggio. Sul metodo marxista della trasformazione sociale*. Feltrinelli.

Negri, A. (1981). *L'anomalia selvaggia : saggio su potere e potenza in Baruch Spinoza*. Feltrinelli.

Negri, A. (1999a). La revolución ha comenzado en 1968. In F. Guattari & A. Negri, *Las verdades nómadas & General Intellect, poder constituyente, comunismo*. Akal.

Negri, A. (1999b). Llamamos comunismo. In F. Guattari & A. Negri, *Las verdades nómadas & General Intellect, poder constituyente, comunismo*. Akal.

Negri, A. (*1999c*). La reacción de los años setenta: no future. In F. Guattari & A. Negri, *Las verdades nómadas & General Intellect, poder constituyente, comunismo*. Akal

Negri, A. (1999d). La nueva alianza. In F. Guattari & A. Negri, *Las verdades nómadas & General Intellect, poder constituyente, comunismo*. Akal.

Negri, A. (1999e). *Insurgencies, Constituent Power and the Modern State*. University of Minnesota Press.

Negri, A. (2000). *Kairòs, alma venus, multitudo. Nove lezioni impartite a me stesso*. Manifestolibri

Negri, A. (2001). *Marx beyond Marx. Lessons on the Grundrisse*. Autonomedia.

Negri, A. (2004). *Los libros de la autonomía obrera*. Akal.

Negri, A. (2004). *La fábrica de la estrategia. 33 lecciones sobre Lenin*. Akal.

Negri, A. (2006). Máquina tiempo, rompecabezas, liberación, constitución. In A. Negri, *Fábricas del sujeto/Ontologías de la subversion*, pp. 13-174. Akal.

Panzieri, R. (1962). Sull'uso capitalista delle macchine nel neocapitalismo. *Quaderni rossi*, 1, 53-72.

Panzieri, R. (1965). Uso socialista della inchiesta operaia. *Quaderni rossi*, 5, 67-76

Panzieri, R. (1977). *La ripresa del marxismo-leninismo in Italia*. Nuove edizioni operaie.

Potier, J. P. (1986). *Lectures italiennes de Marx*. Presse Universitaire de Lyon

Revel, J. (2008). *Vocabulario de Foucault*. Atuel.

Tronti, M. (1962). La fabbrica e la societá. *Quaderni rossi*, 2, 1-31.

Tronti, M. (2019). *Workers and Capital*. Verso.

Trotta, G. & Milana, F. (2008). *L'operaismo degli anni sessanta. Da Quaderni Rossi a Classe Operaia*. DeriveApprodi.

Turchetto, M. (2001). De l'ouvrier masse á l'entrepreneurialité commune: la trajectoire déconcertante de l'operaisme italien. In J. Bidet & E. Kouvélakis (Eds.), *Marx contemporain*. PUF.

Wright, S. (2002). *Storming heaven: class composition and struggle in Italian autonomist Marxism*. Pluto Press

Chapter 7

Open Marxism and class as struggle

Alfonso García Vela

Introduction

Open Marxism views Marx's critical theory as a theory of struggle. Instead of approaching the categories of *Capital* as the objective framework within which class struggle occurs as Marxism has traditionally done, open Marxism claims that class struggle is at the very center of the categories. In other words, class struggle is a constitutive part of social objectivity.

To place class struggle at the center of the analysis is to read *Capital* anew, in a way that is significantly different from other modern interpretations of this text. Interpretations such as the ones by Michael Heinrich (2004) or Moishe Postone (1993), who focus on critically understanding the existence and dynamic of capitalist society. The viewpoint of open Marxism is an attempt to introduce the "real" force of antagonism in the categories, in a way that allows for the understanding of Marx's critical theory as struggle, resistance and rebelliousness of the subjects against the social processes of capitalist domination. Furthermore, unlike the different existing types of relativism, this reading sets thought in motion. It is a rigorous way of thinking which, however, is in constant movement. It opens up the categories to what is new and breaks with the rigidity and formalism that characterizes traditional theory.

In a series of works published during the 1980s and 1990s, John Holloway, Richard Gunn, Werner Bonefeld and Kosmas Psychopedis drew up the general theoretical framework of open Marxism. During these years, open Marxism aspired to being a point of reference which was more radical, profound and critical than the interpretations of Marxian thought by structuralism, the regulation school and analytical Marxism. During the 1990s, John Holloway moved to Mexico and met Sergio Tischler at the Institute of Social Sciences and Humanities of the Autonomous Puebla University, a professor of Guatemalan origin and a former communist militant of the Guatemalan Labor Party (Partido Guatemalteco del Trabajo, PGT). Holloway and Tischler began a dialogue and collaboration that paved the way towards a Latin American branch within open Marxism, which has contributed to its development and renovation.

From the end of the 1990s, important contributions within open Marxism have been made by Ana Cecilia Dinerstein, Sergio Tischler and Alberto Bonnet, aiming at updating Marxism in Latin America through the new forms of anti-capitalist struggle taking place in the region. During the past 20 years, the older members of open Marxism and the Latin American branch have been collaborating closely. Therefore, we could say that the Latin American vision has become an important part of the theoretical production of open Marxism.

The interpretation of Marx's work as a theory of class struggle implies a reflection on the concept of class. For open Marxism, class is a central category for the understanding of present-day struggles and capitalism in general. Its idea of class is a critical approach to the existence of class itself and not its assertion, as viewed by traditional interpretations. This point is very relevant for, as we shall see in more detail further on, the concept of class turns into a critical concept.

In this chapter we will focus on the concept of class within open Marxism and we will try to reconstruct part of the history that led the theorists to take an interest in it. However, before beginning we must ask ourselves: why is it important to tell this story and not only resume the central ideas of open Marxism on the concept of class? The reflections of open Marxism emerged in the 1980s, amidst very adverse historical conditions. They were a group of intellectuals that resisted the crisis affecting Marxism as a result of the defeats of the labor movement around the world and the collapse of the Soviet Union. A crisis from which Marxism has not recovered, not even today. The resistance deployed by these intellectuals is linked with hope in the radical transformation of the world. And hope is a dimension that permeates the work of Marx and resonates in the ideas of open Marxism[1].

Crisis and open Marxism

At the end of the 1980s it was not an easy task to write on the concept of class and class struggle. Orthodox Marxism was collapsing theoretically and politically and this collapse threatened with dragging all currents of Marxist thought down with it. To continue with the theoretical development of Marxism one had to understand that the failure of Marxism was in many ways the failure of orthodox Marxism. And one also had to have an enormous conviction in his critical and analytic potential. For some, the most important feature in Marxism was that its negative critique of bourgeois society showed the possibility of radically changing society. However, at that time everything seemed to be against that possibility.

The 1980s were characterized by the great defeats of the labor movement and the rise and triumph of neoliberalism. And also by the fall of the Berlin wall: this was one of the main events that launched the beginning of the end for the Soviet Union, these historical events had an enormous impact on critical thought. During these years André Gorz (1982) dissolved the centrality of workers as an antagonistic class in his book *Farewell to the Working Class* and Laclau and Mouffe (1985) claimed that we are "now situated in a post-Marxist terrain", where the conception of subjectivity and class elaborated by Marxism could not stand any more. In post-Marxist thought, class appeared as a reductionist and useless concept for understanding today's society. In sum, class was an outdated category that theory had to rid itself of.

However, two years after the end of the mining strike in Great Britain — one of the big defeats of the labor movement which consolidated the government of Margaret Thatcher and promoted neoliberalism in Great Britain — and a few months before the 1987 stock market crash, a Scottish professor at the Edinburgh University called Richard Gunn published an article titled *Notes on Class* in number 2 of journal *Common Sense*. This article set the foundations

---

[1] On the issue of hope in Open Marxism, see Dinerstein (2015).

for a series of very important reflections on the concept of class, developed over a decade later by Werner Bonefeld and John Holloway and later on by Sergio Tischler[2]. These theoretical reflections would constitute the contributions of open Marxism to a theory of class.

At the end of the 1980s there were very few authors that dared write on class and very few academic spaces willing to publish works on this subject. However, *Common Sense* was an alternative space that defied dominant thought and would not let Marxist theory disappear. It was conceived as a Marxist and anarchist journal of theoretical discussion that rejected the model of the university journal and tried to overcome the limitations imposed by a publication. Richard Gunn was one of the founders and main collaborators and the 24 issues published during 12 years included works by Harry Cleaver, Werner Bonefeld, Toni Negri, John Holloway, Mike Rooke, Ana Cecilia Dinerstein, Massimo de Angelis and Kosmas Psychopedis, amongst others. They also hosted letters and communiqués of the Zapatista Army of National Liberation (Ejército Zapatista de Liberación Nacional, EZLN).

The meaning behind the name *Common Sense* constituted an enormous challenge at the end of the 1980s, for this term implied "hope". Hope in the revolutionary transformation of society, a fundamental issue for open Marxism. Hope seemed impossible in a world where the possibilities of a radically new future were falling to pieces and neoliberal capitalism was proclaiming itself as the

---

[2] Sergio Tischler's notion of class struggle is closely linked to his concept of "detotalization", a concept he developed as a critique to the category of totality. Tischler (2007) argues that one of the central categories in the theory of class struggle of Lukács, included in his most important book History and Class Consciousness, is the category of totality. In general terms, for Lukács social totality is a broad, complex, homogeneous and dynamic whole that emerges from labor. Just like Marx, Lukács (1988) claims that capitalism is part of social totality. However, unlike Marx, he states that the totality of capital must be overcome by a new totality embodied by the proletarian class. Using the critique of totality as his foundation, Tischler claims that "detotalization" is a movement in-against-and beyond capital or, in other words, it is a struggle that reclaims the human that is denied by capital. For Tischler, the starting point for thinking class struggle is the negation of totality. Therefore, class struggle is a struggle to detotalize capitalist social relations and detotalization is a "critical concept" of class struggle (Tischler, 2014, p. 332).

only real possibility for humanity. According to Gunn[3], common sense (*sensus comunis*) is an important part of Scottish thought and even more so in 18th-century Scotland, where the term frequently implied two things: a face-to-face coexistence and a human interaction of an oscillatory movement. That is, a coming and going.

The name of the journal comes from its meaning within Scottish thought, although Gunn goes beyond it, influenced by his radical reading of Hegel's *Phenomenology of the Spirit*[4]. So, for Gunn, common sense means a movement that oscillates between human interaction within the limitations of the present world and human interaction in a possible future. In the present, alienated world, interaction is fixed, conformist and tied to consciousness and the restrictions of the unconscious. In a beyond the present world, which is future possibility, interaction is not tied down, it is free and proceeds under its own dynamic. In other words, interaction is egalitarian, free and reciprocal. This oscillatory movement that runs through the present of human interaction and moves towards its future possibility within an emancipated world is the moment of hope that goes beyond the current state of affairs. Despite all that was going on during that decade, Open Marxism did not give up on the hope that it was still possible to radically transform society.

It must be added that, in the 1980s, analytical Marxism was on the rise. This was a theoretical approach that presented itself as an alternative that could rescue Marxism from its crisis and developed influential theories on social classes, such as the class theory of John Roemer or Erik Olin Wright. The school of analytical Marxism set out to turn Marxism into a rigorous social science based on empirical studies, quantitative analysis and the theory of games. According to this perspective, class is fundamentally understood as an empirical and not a critical apitalt, a perspective that is quite different from Marx's thought. In sum, analytical Marxism examines class society but does not go beyond it. On the other hand, as we shall see in what follows, the perspective of Richard Gunn and open

---

[3] Conversations with Richard Gunn.
[4] On this, see Gunn (forthcoming).

Marxism was the complete opposite of what analytical Marxism posited.

Gunn's article "Notes on Class" emerged, on the one hand, as part of a polemic with his friend and colleague John Holloway. From the 1970s, during the times of the German debate on state derivation[5], Holloway underlined the importance of class struggle for the comprehension of the development of capitalist society and criticized the theoretical subordination of class struggle to the objective laws of capital. In fact, for Holloway (1988) the categories of *Capital* are categories of struggle. However, Gunn believed there was a lacuna in Holloway's thought with regard to the concept of class and he wondered what his friend really understood as class.

On the other hand, the article appeared as part of the Marxist debates on class. According to Gunn, for the majority of Marxist writers, be they empirical or structuralist, and even for the non-Marxists, class was basically understood as a group of individuals or as a place that individuals occupied structurally. The groups of individuals are constituted on the basis of something common: for example, their level of earnings, their source of income or their relation with the means of production. Gunn (1987, p. 15) calls this approach, that views classes as groups or places, the sociological conception of class. He claims it is an erroneous interpretation, given that, in the chapter on classes of volume III of *Capital*, Marx rejects this interpretation as mere presupposition.

Indeed, in this chapter, Marx (1971) points out that "at first sight" what allows the specification of a class is the identity of its profit and its source of income. However, he explains that this point of view can lead to an endless division of social groups that would be constituted as different classes. According to Marx (1971, p. 52), if we are to think of class on the basis of this approach, professions would also form classes and "the same would also be true of the infinite fragmentation of interest and rank into which the division of social labor splits laborers as well as capitalists". He points out

---

[5] The state derivation debate was a very important debate within Marxist thought which emerged in West Germany during the 1970s. Its goal was to logically and historically derive the state from the nature of capitalist relations. On this debate, see Clarke (1991), Holloway and Picciotto (1978).

that what truly allows us to say what constitutes a class is to first answer the question of what turns workers and capitalists into social classes. Therefore, the answer to the problem of what a class is cannot be approached on the basis of its forms of appearance as groups or places, because that leads to a fetishized concept of class. For Marx, it must be comprehended on the basis of the social relations that exist behind their forms of appearance, social relations that constitute the worker and the capitalist as classes. This is how Marx analyzes commodity or capital, as social relations and not things, the latter being their fetishized appearance.

In this sense, Gunn points out that class, just as capital, is a social relation and a social relation cannot be a group or a place. This is the starting point for a theory of class and, from there, Gunn claims that class is the relation itself, the antagonistic relation between capital and labor. As a result, class is specifically a relation of struggle. Therefore, class and class relation are exchangeable terms and a class can be conceived as a particular type of class relation. For Gunn (1987, p. 16) thinking of class in terms of struggle does not mean that classes are pre-given social entities that enter in struggle afterward; it means that the fundamental premise of class is class struggle.

E. P. Thompson (1978), one of the most important Marxist historians, posited a similar interpretation. For this author, the concept of class cannot be separated from the notion of class struggle. From a historical analysis, Thompson claims that in the process of struggle subjects are revealed as a class. Therefore, class struggle as a concept pre-exists that of class. According to Thompson, in the real historical process class and class consciousness are always the last phases of this process, not the first. However, Gunn (1987, p. 16) tries to go beyond this approach when he states that class struggle is intrinsic to class. That is, struggle does not exist before class as Thompson points out, "class struggle is class itself". This is one of the most important contributions of his article and, according to Gunn, this is the way in which Marx introduces class at the beginning of the *Communist Manifesto*. In the *Communist Manifesto*, the emphasis is put on class struggle as a social dynamic that is at the center of "the history of all hitherto existing society"[6].

Gunn calls the approach that conceives class as a relation of struggle the Marxist notion of class. In his article, he shows the differences that exist between this notion and the sociological conception of class. In showing the differences between the two approaches, Gunn tries to unveil the limits of the sociological conception of class and elucidate the theoretical and practical consequences of embracing the Marxist or the sociological notion of class. The following are the differences I considered to be crucial:

Firstly, due to its interpretation of class as groups or places, the sociological conception is confronted with the difficulty that not all individuals can be located within the capitalist or the proletarian class. To escape this difficulty, the sociological conception is forced to turn to residual categories such as the middle classes or the middle strata. For Gunn (1987, p. 17), these are the theoretical figments of an impoverished conceptual scheme. This perspective implies a powerful critique to the theory of Erik Olin Wright (1985) on middle classes and the overall conceptualization of their class structure as a set of positions occupied by individuals and families. Unlike the sociological conception, the Marxist notion does not face this difficulty for it considers that the capital-labor relation structures the concrete life of individuals qualitatively, quantitatively and antagonistically, and that this structuring of lives is expressed in different ways.

Secondly, in the Marxist notion the pure worker or the pure capitalist are not methodologically privileged. That is, the capitalist and the worker are treated as limit cases and considered as figures that intertwine with others in "a diversely structured crowd" (1987, p. 18). In the sociological conception, the pure worker and the pure capitalist are treated as methodological pillars for the formation of the intermediate classes. According to Gunn there is no pure proletariat for Marx, given that in bourgeois society the producer of surplus value is permeated by the salary relation in which the ideological mystification is inherent. That is, although the worker lives the

---

[6] Paragraph quoted from the *Communist Manifesto* (Marx & Engels, 1848/1976).

experience of capitalist exploitation, he/she is permeated by the bourgeois ideology against him/herself.

In the third place, for the Marxist notion there is a unique class relation that structures the lives of individuals: the capital-labor relation. The sociological conception, on the contrary, recognizes multiple ways in which groups or places might possibly relate to each other. Gunn (1987, p. 19) points out that, despite the fact that the Marxist conception of class is accused of being reductionist, it is actually not. It shows "the experiential richness of individuals' (self)-contradictory life-texture into full theoretical and phenomenological light", while the sociological conception does succumb to reductionism, for it wants to place each individual into some kind of group or specific place, leaving aside the existence of the trans-categorical individual. Furthermore, the Marxist notion of class does not construct class in terms of roles as the sociological conception does. The definition of roles is not a methodological principle. On the contrary, the Marxist conception of class shows the very struggle of the individual that permanently questions the universal and particular dimensions of individuality. According to Gunn, the definition of roles as proletarian or bourgeois is not a theoretical or practical solution for Marx, but rather a theoretical problem that must be solved.

Finally, according to Gunn, the interpretation of the concept of class as groups or places opens up a broad spectrum of classes and class fractions. Therefore, political practice has to do with alliances between classes and fractions. Furthermore, given that the sociological conception attributes a privileged or leading role to the pure working class, a hierarchical vision of class struggle is established. This leads to the idea of the party as a vanguard and to the distinction between advanced or retrograde class elements. Gunn points out that the Marxist notion of class breaks with this vision of political practice. On the one hand, given there is only one class relation this notion does not raise a question of alliances between classes and class fractions. On the other hand, in the Marxist notion the pure working class has no privileged political place, for such a place does not exist. The result is the destruction of all idea of a vanguard party. Thus, for Gunn (1987, p. 21) "authentic Marxist politics amounts to politics in an anarchistic mode". The critique of the Leninist idea of the vanguard party is crucial for open Marxism due to its importance in the updating of the concept of revolution and political practice. In Gunn's article we find some of the pillars of this critique, developed later on in the work of Sergio Tischler (2003, 2007).

Gunn's analysis unveils the limitations of sociological Marxism, whose most conspicuous representative at that moment was analytical Marxism. Furthermore, it shows that class was not a reductionist or outdated concept as the post-Marxists argued, it was still a central category for the comprehension of present-day capitalism. As he himself underlines at the end of his article, Gunn's (1987, p. 24) approach frees class analysis from all determinism, for at the center of analysis lies the "finely-textured and continually and unpredictably developing struggle which, for Marx, is the existence of class per se". In this sense, Gunn's theoretical position and that of open Marxism was clearly a struggle in conceptual terms that opened up the possibility of a radical transformation of society despite the collapse of real socialism and the apparent triumph of neoliberal capitalism. Finally, Richard Gunn states that when he finished his article Notes on Class he realized there was no gap in the conception of class of his friend John Holloway. On the contrary, the notion of class that Holloway defended in their conversations was correct and Gunn was therefore convinced about the conceptions of his friend.

Constitution and existence

During the 1990s, open Marxism continued with its theoretical reflection and resisted the enormous impact that the end of real socialism had on critical thought, the great diffusion of Fukuyama's thesis on the end of history and Derrida's (1994) claim that Marx had died and the utopia had died with him. These events caused real concern on the death of Marxism, expressed by Holloway in his article "The Relevance of Marxism Today" (1994, p. 40): "When I use Marxist categories now, I often have the impression that I am speaking Latin, that I am speaking an ancient language that few people understand, a language that may soon be dead". However, Holloway transcends the pessimism that infuses the beginning of his article and expresses a social reality. He does"not renounce today's relevance of Marxism as a theory that provides the foundations for a radical critique of this society of domination, exploitation and death.

Furthermore, a series of protests and rebellions broke out in the 1990s against neoliberal capitalism, such as the *143apitalis* uprising, the general strike in France and the battle of Seattle. These struggle gave new impulse to critical thought and shook the foundations of the discourse on the end of history and the death of Marx. In this historical context, Werner Bonefeld, one of the prominent members of open Marxism, produced a significant reflection on the concept of class. Werner Bonefeld obtained his degree in political science from the Free University of Berlin. Johannes Agnoli, his professor, had a great impact on his thought. For Bonefeld (2004), Agnoli was the thinker of human dignity as well as the practical theorist of 1968 in West Germany. After completing his studies in Berlin, Bonefeld moved to Edinburgh University and conducted his doctorate studies under the direction of John Holloway; Richard Gunn was also highly involved in his thesis. From that point on, Bonefeld, Gunn and Holloway began an intense intellectual collaboration that continues until today.

Bonefeld's approach to class comes from his effort to link his interpretation of original or primitive accumulation to the concept of class[7]. He had previously tried to conceptualize the meaning of original accumulation in the constitution of capitalist social relations. His concern for original accumulation began with the article *Class struggle and the permanence of primitive accumulation*, published in 1998 in number 6 of *Common Sense*.

The core of his argument (1988, 2001), developed in later articles, is that original accumulation does not only describe the period of transition that led from feudalism to the emergence of capitalism. In fact, original accumulation understood as the separation of the producer from the means of production describes a process that is

---

[7] Conversations with Werner Bonefeld.

permanently reproduced throughout the history of capital. According to Bonefeld (2001, 2013), the Marxist tradition has wrongly understood primitive accumulation as the prehistory of capitalism. The separation between the producer and the means of production is interpreted as a consolidated fact that belongs to the past. However, the history of capital until today shows that the accumulation and expansion of capital entail a constant separation between the producer and the means of production. Therefore, for Bonefeld, original accumulation is the precondition and "ongoing premise" of capitalist social relations. Its relevance resides in that it is a "c"ntrifugal point" around which the existence of social work in capitalism is resolved.

Bonefeld's position on the permanence of original accumulation is quite disputable due to the complexity of the very concept of primitive accumulation. It does not only imply the separation of the producer from the means of production, it also encompasses the conditions and historical premises that existed before capital and within which the first separation between the producer and the means of production took place. It must be stressed that Bonefeld correctly points out that the premise or constitutive assumption of capital is not a consolidated fact that belongs to capital's past, it is a continuous process of constitution. This implies a struggle of us against the reconstitution of the separation. Said formulation is one of Bonefeld's most important contributions, referring to the relation between constitution and existence, a relation that is particularly relevant in Open Marxism.

What open Marxism posits is that the existence of the capitalist forms of social relations (such as the commodity, money, the state, etc.) is not radically separated from their constitution or genesis. That is, the genesis of these forms or the process that constituted their existence is not a historical past that is concluded and temporally separated from its existence. On the contrary, constitution and existence are intrinsically linked. Therefore, existence is interpreted as a permanent struggle of capital against humanity for the constitution and reconstitution of social relations of domination[8].

---

[8] On the relation between constitution and existence, see Holloway (2002).

On the basis of his reflections on original accumulation and the ideas of Gunn on the concept of class, Bonefeld established a connection between class and primitive accumulation in an article titled *Class and Constitution*. This article was first written as a presentation for congress *The Labor Debate*, organized in February 1999 by Ana C. Dinerstein and Michael Neary at Warwick University in England[9]. It was published in Spanish in 2001 in number 2 of journal *Bajo el Volcán*.

In this article, Bonefeld rejects all efforts to define class. He argues (2005) that definitions are static and depend on pre-existing notions on society, from which subjects and their roles are derived. A definition of class risks becoming tautological and contradictory. Therefore, the comprehension of the concept of class "cannot advance as an exercise of definitions", this approach remains anchored to a reified world. If Bonefeld's theoretical project is to stress dynamic social relations, it must go beyond static and classifying definitions. Therefore, to understand class one must conceptualize; and to conceptualize means, for our author, to determine; and to determine is to "question the constitution and social movement of a reified world" (Bonefeld, 2003). In this sense, critical theory can be understood as a theory of determination. On the contrary, a theory of class that is constructed on the basis of definitions is part of a sociological conception or a sociological Marxism. Just like analytical Marxism which, for Bonefeld, is no more than another mode of appearance of Marxism-Leninism.

Following Marx, Bonefeld argues that in order to say what a class is, one must first answer the question of what it is that turns wage workers into a social class. At the center of the answer provided by Bonefeld's theory is "the permanence of original accumulation" or, in other words, the continuous separation of labor from its conditions. Bonefeld reclaims the issue of the constitution of capitalist social relations in order to understand class, an issue that is crucial for Marx and that the tradition of sociological Marxism has set aside.

---

[9] Conversation with Werner Bonefeld. On the Labor Debate, see the book by Dinerstein and Neary (2002).

According to Bonefeld, the separation of labor from its means is no longer the condition for the historical emergence of capital. It has turned into the constitutive presupposition of its existence. Consequently, original accumulation is also the foundation of social classes in capitalism. In other words, the separation between the producer and the means of production is the condition for the existence of the worker and of the capitalist as classes. However, this separation was the result of the class struggle that liberated the master from the serf and the serf from the master. In this sense, for Bonefeld just as for Gunn, class struggle is the fundamental premise of class.

So, for Bonefeld (s/n), class is a dynamic social relation whose constitutive existence is the separation of labor from its conditions. When Bonefeld founds the existence of class on separation, he tries to show that the comprehension of social relations cannot be based on "*a priori* notions" or on the established existence of the working class and the capitalist class. It is based on their constitution or genesis and it is only through there that we can understand the existence of class. Hence, historical constitution is the starting point for the understanding of class struggle.

As Bonefeld argues, these approaches imply that the category of class makes sense only as a critical category. For if the existence of capitalist social relations is understood as something finished or established, without theorizing the constitutive relation of the separation, the working class would be interpreted in terms of its assertion and not its negation. So, for Bonefeld (s/n), "class is not an affirmative category but a critical concept". In sum, the working class is the class that struggles against its own existence as a class. Therefore, for open Marxism the overcoming of capitalism would imply the abolition of the proletariat and not its self-realization.

As we will see in the following section, the arguments of Richard Gunn and Werner Bonefeld had a great impact on John Holloway's conception of class. However, we can say that there was a mutual illumination between these authors, which led to a collective theoretical project on the notion of class. The article by Holloway that we will analyze in what follows, *Class and Classification*, was presented at the congress *The Labor Debate*. This article expressed the impulse given to critical theory by neoliberal capitalism. It emerged from the need to reflect on whether these struggles were new forms of class struggle.

Fetishization and Class

In *Class and Classification*, Holloway approaches the effect that understanding fetishism as a process of fetishization has on the concept of class. For our author, there are two different ways of understanding fetishism. On the one hand, there is the conception of fetishism as an established fact; on the other, fetishization as a continuous struggle to fetishize. The discussion on fetishism and fetishization is highly relevant for Holloway. In *Change the World Without Taking Power*, one of his most important books published a few years later, this discussion is central for his critique of the state and capital. More recently (2013), he argued that nouns suggest a certain crystallization and exclude the active social subject, while verbs express movement, action and openness.

Holloway points out that in certain paragraphs of *Capital* Marx seems to describe fetishism as an accomplished, fixed fact. This conception has important consequences in theory and practice. Firstly, if social relations are assumed to be indeed fetishized, a distinction is established between the working class and the theorists. The theorists are considered as the subjects that can penetrate the fetishized appearances of social relations and understand reified social relations as the historically specific mode of existence of relations between people. This leads to a conception of theorists as the illuminated subjects who are capable of guiding the workers who live in a fetishized world. It turns theory into something elitist and theoretically eliminates the possibility of the self-emancipation of workers.

Secondly, if fetishism is interpreted as an established fact, the domination that implies fetishized social relations is taken for granted. Therefore, social existence within capitalism is determined by domination and not by class struggle and Marxism turns into a theory of social domination. Thirdly, if fetishism is a consummated, fixed fact, this means the fetishized forms were constituted at the genesis of capitalism. Their constitution is interpreted as a historical past that is temporally separated from their existence, meaning that constitution and existence are separated. As we have already pointed out, this is very problematic for open Marxism.

Likewise, the conception of fetishism as a done fact has crucial consequences for the notion of class. For Holloway (2011), a big part of the Marxist debates on the concept of class take the establishment of the fetishized forms for granted. Therefore, the relation between the capitalist class and the working class is considered a relation of domination of capital over labor. This is the basis for the efforts to define the working class and study its struggle. That is, the subordination of labor to capital offers the possibility to define the working class. Consequently, subordination opens the way to definition and, for Holloway and the other members of *open Marxism*, definitions close the world even more.

Additionally, definitions lead to the identification of class as groups of people and, as we have already seen, open Marxism considers that classes are neither groups nor places. Holloway points out that the process of identification or classification is the starting point for discussions between Marxists on whether a movement is a class movement or not. Also, classification leads to the problem of belonging. If we are to assume a pre-established definition of class, we must place ourselves or other people within the pre-existing definitions of class. But that is not a simple endeavor. What class does Marx belong to? Or the *zapatistas*? Or the feminists? And so on.

There is another problem that emerges from the definition of class and that is the definition of struggles. Holloway (2004) points out that the characterization of struggles is derived from the definition of class. The individual who has defined the class also specifies the relevance of the antagonism of struggles, whether it is valid or not. This can lead to the obscuring of the perception of class antagonism and to the conclusion that class struggle is no longer important for social change.

However, Holloway (2011) points out that if fetishism is understood as an active process of fetishization, this means that social relations are contradictory whether they are fetishized or not. Fetishism is presented as a struggle between the constant process of fetishization of social relations and anti-fetishizing tendencies. According to this approach, fetishization and struggle are not separated. Therefore, capitalist domination is not complete, it is a "struggle to fetishize" and "the present existence of social forms is their ever-renewed constitution". Therefore, constitution and existence are united and the production of social relations is always in dispute.

On this basis, Holloway (2011) points out that "capitalism is the ever renewed generation of class, the ever renewed classification of people". To posit the existence of classes means that these are in a permanent process of constitution. Following Bonefeld's analysis, Holloway argues that class can be seen as the violent separation between the subject and the object. In capitalism, the obje't that has been created and produced by the subject is confiscated every day. The violence of this appropriation is not an exclusive characteristic of original accumulation, it is a fundamental part of the existence of capitalism: the capitalist class and the working class cannot exist without the separation between the subject and the object. Therefore, this separation is constitutive of class and of the classification of humanity.

For Holloway (2011), class struggle is "the struggle to classify and against being classified at the same time as it is, indistinguishably, the struggle between constituted classes". From this perspective, class conflict does not occur after the establishment of the subordination of labor to capital or the constitution of classes, it is a conflict between subordination and insubordination. Thus, class struggle is a struggle to constitute capitalist social relations. To sum up, for Holloway the constitution of capitalist social relations is in itself class struggle. Here we can observe the mutual influence between Holloway and Gunn: For Gunn, class struggle is class itself. In the words of Holloway, the very constitution of class is a struggle.

Holloway's approach (2011) is broader and more profound than classic Marxist theories, according to which what characterized a struggle as revolutionary depended on whether or not it was the struggle of the working class. Holloway claims "we do not struggle *as* working class, we struggle *against* being working class, against being classified". In this sense, what matters in class struggle is not if we are or not the working class. What matters is the struggle against the process of fetishization, against capitalist classification and against our being working class. That is what gives unity to the struggles and not the fact of being or not members of a same class. To sum up, for our author struggle is not born out of the fact that we are the working class; being the working class does not amount to being a revolutionary class. The struggle emerges from our existence in-against-and beyond being the working class.

Finally, Holloway (2011) suggests we cannot understand capitalism simply in terms of the contradiction between labor and capital, we must understand labor as a constitutive element of capitalist social relations. "Labor is the production of capital and the production of capital is the production of class, classification". However, labor exists within capitalism in a contradictory mode. It can be understood as the form of existence of voluntary or creative activity or, to put it differently, doing. To assert that doing exists as labor, implies that it also exists as anti-labor. Hence, class struggle is the struggle of doing against labor, it is the struggle for the self-determination of doing.

Conclusion

Open Marxism tells us that the key to understanding class is to approach it in negative or critical terms. Class is the negation of class itself, it is the very struggle of people against their being a class, against being classified. Therefore, class is struggle: this is one of the most important contributions of open Marxism. Furthermore, it must be stressed that its concept of class is linked to the struggles for human emancipation and seeks to enter in dialogue with them.

Open Marxism underlines that if we want to think in critical terms, we cannot separate class and struggle. When they are separated, class is conceived affirmatively as groups or places. This causes many problems and pertains to a Marxist tradition that accepts social relations as something constituted, as fixed facts. For open Marxism this perspective is fetishist in itself, given that the separation of struggle results in the exclusion of the active social subject and the concealment of struggles that exist behind the fetishized forms of capital, such as class, money, the state or the party. To see the struggles, one must criticize the fetishized appearance of social relations.

For open Marxism, class struggle cannot be conceived as a conflict between two separate groups of people. Class struggle is a conflict that runs through the totality of capitalist social relations, including class itself.

Now then, why is the concept of class relevant today? Open Marxism basically answers that class allows us to see the unity underlying the diversity of today's struggles and, at the same time, it addresses us as active subjects, as subjects struggling for the social self-determination of their own doing. To sum up, open Marxism updates the concept of class and breaks with the classic cannon of class struggle. It shows us that the idea of class expresses our capacity to resist capital and our power to transform the world.

Translated by Anna-Maeve Holloway

References

Bonefeld, W. (1988). Class struggle and the permanence of primitive accumulation. *Common Sense* 6, 54–65.

Bonefeld, W. (2004). Farewell Johannes. *Capital & Class* 28(2), 167–177.

Bonefeld, W. (2005). *Capital, labor and Primitive Accumulation*. Retrieved from https://libcom.org/library/capital-labor-and-primitive-accumulation

Bonefeld, W. (2001). The permanence of primitive accumulation: commodity, fetishism and social constitution *The Commoner*, 2

Bonefeld, W. (2013). *La razón corrosiva: una crítica al Estado y al capital*. Herramienta.

Clarke, S. (Ed.). (1991). *The State debate*. Macmillan.

Derrida, J. (1994) *Specters of Marx: The state of the debt, the work of mourning and the new international*. Routledge.

Dinerstein, A. C. & Neary, M. (eds.) (2002) *The labor Debate: An Investigation into the Theory and Reality of Capitalist Work*. Ashgate.

Dinerstein, A. C. (2015). *The politics of autonomy in Latin America. The art of organizing hope.* Palgrave Macmillan.

Engels, F., & Marx, K. (1848/1976) The Communist Manifesto. In K. Marx & F. Engels, *Collected Works, Vol. 6, 1845–1848.* Lawrence & Wishart.

Gorz, A. (1982) *Farewell to the Working Class.* Pluto Press.

Gunn, R. (1987). Notes on Class. *Common Sense* 2, 15–25.

Gunn, R. (forthcoming). *Five Lectures on Hegel.* PM Press.

Heinrich, M. (2004). *An Introduction to the Three Volumes of Karl Marx's Capital.* Monthly Review Press.

Holloway, J. (1988). The Great Bear: Post-Fordism and Class Struggle. *Capital and Class* 36, 88–92.

Holloway, J. (1994). The relevance of Marxism today. *Common Sense* 15, 38–42.

Holloway, J. (1994b). *Marxism, State and Capital.* Editorial Tierra del Fuego.

Holloway, J. (2011). Class and Classification. Retrieved at http://www.johnholloway.com.mx/2011/07/30/class-and-classification/

Holloway, J. (2002). *Change the World Without Taking Power.* Pluto Press.

Holloway, J. (2010) *Crack Capitalism.* Pluto Press.

Holloway, J. (2013). *¡Comunicemos!.* Grietas Editores.

Holloway, J. & Picciotto, S. (Eds.). (1978). *State and Capital. A Marxist debate.* Edward Arnold.

Laclau, E. & Moufe, C. (1985). *Hegemony and Social Strategy. Towards a Radical Democratic Politics.* Verso.

Lukács, G. (1988*). History and Class Consciousness: Studies in Marxist Dialectics.* MIT Press.

Marx, K. (1894/1971) *Capital, Vol. 3.* Lawrence & Wishart.

Postone, M. (1993). *Time, labor and Social Domination. A reinterpretation of Marx's Critical Theory.* Cambridge University Press.

Roemer, J. (1986). Rational choice Marxism. Some issues of method and substance. In J. Roemer (Ed.), *Analytical Marxism* (pp. 191–201). Cambridge University Press.

Roemer, J. (1994). *A future for Socialism.* Harvard University Press.

Thompson, E. P. (1978). Eighteenth Century English Society: Class Struggle Without Class? *Social History* 3(2)

Tischler, S. (2003). The crisis of the Leninist subject and the Zapatista circumstance. In S. Tischler & W. Bonefeld (Eds.) *What is to be Done?: New Times and the Anniversary of a Question.* Ashgate Publishing Group.

Tischler, S. (2007) Adorno: The Conceptual Prison of the Subject, Political Fetishism and Class Struggle. In J. Holloway, F. Matamoros, & S. Tischler (Eds.), *Negativity and Revolution*. Pluto Press.

Tischler, S. (2012). Revolution and Detotalization. *Journal of Classical Sociology* 12(2), 267–280.

Tischler, S. (2014). Detotalization and Subject. On Zapatismo and Critical Theory. *South Altantic Quarterly* 113(2), 327–338.

Wright, E.O. (1985) *Classes*. Verso.

Wright, E.O. & Fung, A. (Eds.). (2003). *Deepening Democracy. Institutional innovations in empowered participatory governance*. Verso.

Chapter 8

Final reflections: on the sociological relevance of the Marxist concept of social class

Massimo Modonesi

The foundation of Marxist thought has as its touchstone the most basic, well-known, and problematic concept in all of Marxism: class struggle. Just as we can recognize in Marxism a principle of intelligibility related to the logic of capital, it is necessary not to lose sight of a second principle linked to the logic of the class struggle, hidden by and subordinated to the first in the works of Marx and his successors (Dardot & Laval, 2012, p. 219).

The theoretical perspective that emerged from this conceptual apparatus was so influential as to be hegemonic during most of the 20th century, only to later be considered obsolete at the end of the century. As Goran Therborn rightly notes: "The recently philosophy of struggle without classes corresponds to the sociology of classes without struggle" (Therborn, 2014, p. 157).

In what follows I will offer some coordinates that allow us to reclaim this idea and its theoretical implications from the perspective of political sociology, rather than (as is more commonly the case) political strategy, history, or philosophy, of the kind dealt with in Domenico Losurdo's recent book, *Class Struggle* (2013).

I will not be able here to analyze the set of questions and hypotheses that arise from these concepts, nor, most importantly, the relationship between them, with the depth they deserve. It is my hope that the following arguments serve as an exercise in conceptual problematization and an invitation to the debate.

I.

Social class should not be understood as an isolated and static concept, but a dynamic and relational one, inserted in the formula of *class struggle*.

The central hypothesis that I developed in a recent book[1] is that identifying, describing, analyzing, explaining, and interpreting struggles, classes, and the forms and circumstances of their intersection, under the assumption that struggles are class struggles and that classes struggle, is the essential core of a Marxist theory of political action. A theory centered in the antagonistic principle.

There is a certain consensus around the idea that there is simultaneity and synchrony between the construction of subjectivity and the action that shapes and expresses it. However, the Marxist debate polarized between those that defended the primacy of one over the other; structure vs action, class-in-itself vs class-for-itself. These different perspectives led to different sequences.

An approach that favors struggle is clearly and explicitly evident, for instance, in three analytical interpretations included in this book: E.P. Thompson, Italian *operaismo,* and open Marxism. The words of E.P. Thompson are a good illustration of this intense and fecund debate, which is not exempt from substantial deviations and controversies:

> "In my view, far too much theoretical attention (much of it plainly ahistorical) has been paid to 'class', and far too little to 'class struggle'. Indeed, class struggle is the prior, as well as the more universal, concept. To put it bluntly: classes do not exist as separate entities, look around, find an enemy class, and then start to struggle. On the contrary, people find themselves in a society structured in determined ways (crucially, but not exclusively, in productive relations), they experience exploitation (or the need to maintain power over those whom they exploit), they identify points of antagonistic interest, they commence to struggle around these issues and in the process of struggling they discover themselves as classes, they come to know this discovery as class-consciousness. Class and class-consciousness are always the last, not the first, stage in the real historical process. But if we employ a static category of class, or if we derive our concept from a prior theoretical model of a structural totality, we will not suppose so: we will suppose that class is

---

[1] See Modonesi (2018). Many of the arguments in this chapter were presented in that text.

instantaneously present (derivative, like a geometric projection, from productive relations) and that hence classes struggle (Thompson, 1978, p. 149).

Indeed, the Marxist notion of struggle allows for the opening of an array of questions related to action that includes the dimension of what sociologists call *agency*: questions about who actors and subjects are and how they organize themselves and enter into conflict. In this approach, struggle is the dynamic and evolutionary substance in the formula *class struggle*.

On the other hand, with respect to temporality, the Marxist notion of struggle encompasses and allows for the inclusion of the process as well as the event, and invites a consideration of the relationship between the two. This is not only a quantitative question of whether it is short-, medium-, or long-term, but also a qualitative one: a question that allows us to emphasize continuous, cumulative periods, with ruptures, discontinuities, and historical shocks[2].

Finally, the concept of *struggle* poses the question of strategy, in which the confrontation between classes turns political and the subjective dimension of antagonism surfaces. Struggle is social, to the extent that it is unleashed in society, and political, insofar as it is a dispute over power. In this way, the internal construction of class is carried out based on struggle, with class struggle as the battlefield, the context for the conflict specific to capitalist societies. The collective and the subjective are forged in struggle, socially and politically located in the situation of class; the confrontation is much more than a *structural effect* or the simple *condition* or *situation of class*.

Marxism thus aims at a specific form of social action, a political action that is a class action and an antagonistic action. In this task it has a perspective and establishes an analytical logic of mobilization, of emerging struggles, framed by class, whose tendency is to become political.

---

[2] For a reading of Marx that recalls the intuitions of Walter Benjamin and Ernst Bloch regarding non-linear temporalities, see Bensaid (2010).

II.

The notion of *class*, inasmuch as it contains a determining element of socioeconomic reality, is a powerful antidote against the postmodern culturalism, politicism, and subjectivism that run through the dominant approaches in the study of social movements.

At the same time, although the concept of class in its sociopolitical strain has been de-objectified and de-fetishized by critical Marxisms, it retains a stake in conceptualizing the political on the basis of aggregation and collective action on a level prior to and outside of the state, without excluding a subsequent development in that direction. Thus, class is (also) a concept of political theory. At its heart are some tensions and possible hypotheses of articulation. Indeed, the notion of class is, in Marxist terms, a synthesis of the dialectical relation between material socioeconomic determination and sociopolitical subjectivation, a notion that has one foot in structure and the other in agency, simultaneously class-in-itself and class-for-itself.

For this reason, in the search for a meeting point between Marxism and the new critical sociologies (in particular that of Bourdieu), Philippe Corcuff and Daniel Bensaid emphasize the perspective of constructivism, which in the case of Marxism translates into a conception of class, the subject, and the actor in general as constructors and constructs. This is also a clear attempt to avoid the polarity and the dualism of object-subject (Corcuff, 2001, pp. 18–20; Bensaid, 2005, p. 32).

On another level, conceiving of class as a '*field*' or a 'universe of class' allows for the recognition and analysis of a series of sociopolitical processes of aggregation[3] without falling into the essentialism of a certain workerism dating from an era marked by the

---

[3] The notion of field does not refer here to the thinking of Pierre Bourdieu, who by the way adopts a peculiar class perspective that recovers, by means of the habitus, the idea of an incorporation of specific and distinguishable forms, but does not order or clearly hierarchize the economic, political, and cultural conditions. Neither does it consider the possibility of a political conscience and praxis—and with it, a fault line in the habitus—that does not deny the forms of daily reproduction and a political bifurcation between subordination and insubordination, subalternity, and antagonism.

centrality of the industrial worker—or a search for new immaterial centralities. This approach also has the merit of not avoiding the fact that contemporary social reality continues to be marked by the logic of capital and private ownership of the means of production, the exploitation of workers, and the dispossession of *the commons*. In this sense, class does not exist as a single sociopolitical entity; there is a field of classes and class struggles in which subjectivities and actors emerge and are shaped. As Colin Barker argues, social movements in this sense are mediations of the class struggle (Barker, 2013, p. 47).

Indeed, we should not forget that apart from the subjectively anticapitalist nature of struggles, their class nature puts the question of struggle in the context of capitalism on an objective level. The notion of class requires an understanding of conflict based on certain readings that situate it in the framework of the capital-labor relationship, understood as a matrix that may not describe all of the causes and aims of struggles, but which nonetheless constitutes an unavoidable starting point[4]. A class vision of capitalist societies and sociopolitical phenomena does not preclude recognition of other contradictions and antagonisms related to questions such as gender oppression, national liberation, or the race question. On the contrary, only a class perspective allows for the recognition of the imbrications and tensions that articulate, bind, fragment, or dissociate different social, political, and cultural cleavages.

The alternative, that is, the negation of the class dimension in relation to the phenomena of mobilization, means denying that structural position and material objectification fulfil a social role. The principle of class analysis avoids a collapse into culturalist explanations as well as a drift into the mere study of the forms of social movements and redirects the problem back to the content or, if you will, the foundation.

Along these lines, Burawoy and Wright maintain that the concept of exploitation and the class analysis of the social relations of

---

[4]   As, for example, the problem of the decisional squares and sphere as a dimension that makes class structure and its political projection more complex. On this topic, as well as the school of Wright's analytic Marxism, see Bidet and Dumenil (2007).

production in capitalist societies form the conceptual core of Marxist sociology. At the same time, they recognize that the exploited retain a certain power of resistance to exploitation, which poses a challenge to the social reproduction of capitalism (Burawoy & Wright, 2000). In this sense, Mezzadra recognizes in Marx a "subjective excess", that is, "the excess of the subject with respect to the conditions of restraint" (Mezzadra, 2014, p. 131). Raymond Williams formulates this idea clearly as follows:

> "What has really to be said, as a way of defining important elements of both the residual and the emergent, and as a way of understanding the character of the dominant, is that no mode of production and therefore no dominant social order and therefore no dominant culture ever in reality includes or exhausts all human practice, human energy, and human intention" (Williams, 1977, p. 125).

In this sense, class traces itself in its centrality as a political subjectivity hand in hand with the principle of *praxis*, at a point of intersection between being and consciousness.

> "Classes arise because men and women, in determinate productive relations, identify their antagonistic interests, and come to struggle, to think, and to value in class ways: thus the process of class formation is a process of self-making, although under conditions which are 'given'" (Thompson, 1995, p. 143).

Ellen Meiksins Wood, recalling Thompson's intuitions, argues that the notion of class is more fertile when it is conceived historically as a relationship, as a process, and, I would add, as a crucible of social and political movements (Wood, 2013, pp. 90–126). Between experience and practice, consciousness and spontaneity, class subjectivity emerges as a "disposition to act"[5].

---

[5] "Class is a social and cultural formation (often finding institutional expression) which cannot be defined abstractly, or in isolation, but only in terms of relationship with other classes; and, ultimately, the definition can only be made in the medium of time—that is, action and reaction, change and conflict. When we speak of a class we are thinking of a very loosely defined body of people who share the same congeries of interests, social experiences, traditions and value-system, who have a disposition to behave as a class, to define themselves in their actions and in their consciousness in relation to other groups of people in class ways. But class itself is not a thing, it is a happening" (Thompson, 1965, p. 357).

III.

We know that one of the problematic and therefore fertile elements of the Marxist debate is the issue of *class consciousness*. Without trying to synthesize this debate here, I will point out some elements that can be considered conventional, that is, relatively accepted and therefore part of a possible general definition. In Marxism, *consciousness* corresponds in broad terms to what is currently known in cultural sociology as *identity*, except that it is not reduced to the cultural dimension, but refers directly and explicitly to the concrete layer of class as social and material referent and translates directly into political attitude and behavior. This connection does not imply that they are entirely the same, since we cannot overlook the specific political situation or the tension-articulation between social being and consciousness, which does not resolve simply into a self-representation of the subject. Drawing on the elements proposed by Thompson, class consciousness would be the perception — understood as identification and recognition — of the experience of exploitation and domination in an external relationship of differentiation and confrontation with class antagonists, with an internal link of articulation and group solidarity, as well as in collective representation and worldview — that is, in *ideology*.

The question of consciousness is connected, via the 'spirit of scission', with the question of autonomy considered as a rupture with domination, as a principle of independence and self-determination of class, which also, on the subjective and cultural level, refers to the capacity of self-representation (Bihr, 2012, p. 102.). Indeed, in Marxist debate the concept of autonomy is also a synonym of independent organization, of class independence in the operative and political sense. Historically and theoretically, class is a social field, but also a political field in which networks are woven, militant paths are constructed, and union and party organizations are built. In this sense, social movements arise on the terrain of class[6]. The militant, and not the worker, is the unit or atom of class analysis

---

[6] As opposed to when it was considered, in a discursive simplification with multiple ideological implications, that class formed the workers' movement and that this was the social movement.

understood and thought of as the field of sociopolitical movements, of antagonist movements.

The question of organization at the heart of class leads to the question of the political party, and more specifically to the connection between the *ephemeral* party, understood as a specific organization, and the *historical* party, conceived as a general movement (Marx 1860). This involves a series of qualities and indispensable political functions that give the class cohesion and protection, most concretely to those parts that are already mobilized. Critical Marxism has understood the *political party*—apart from bureaucratic degenerations and past and present particracies—as a fundamental instance of politicization, of collective consolidation of the impulse to solidarity and social cooperation between different expressions of the working class; it has been seen as an instance of the accumulation of experience and historical memory, of political education, of political and strategic orientation and direction. At the same time, but on another level, it is important to remember the Marxist criticisms—Luxemburgist, council communist, Autonomist Marxist—founded on the idea that the party was a concept prone to degeneration, and particularly to bureaucratization and authoritarianism disguised as "democratic centralism".

From the perspective of the party or parties organized by class, the question of social movements, understood as plurality and diversity, leaves open a series of political questions. For example, for Daniel Bensaid, it is essential to maintain unity between the "plurality and relative autonomy" of the field, capital, and domination with a strategic "relative unity" (Bensaid, 2005, p. 4). And it is precisely the notion of class that allows one to think, in a Marxist vein, about the passages from the particular to the general that run through the political and the cultural, as well as the tension between pluralism and unity and between universality and difference. Class, as a backbone concept in the Marxist sociology of political action, is positioned as a general framework for the processes of politicization, of importance to politics and the universalization of struggle.

At the same time, as a key to sociological interpretation, we must keep open the possibility of disaggregating the notion of *class struggle* in the analysis of concrete political movements. As much as class struggle refers to a starting point for analyzing movements under capitalism, we must ask how to articulate this proposal within the singularity of movements and the different forms of action presented by classes through their concrete fractions in their daily sociopolitical action. That is, following the path of Marx's own historical analyses, class struggle in a specific time and place means specific inter- and intra-class conflicts that are manifested in different inter- and intra-class alliances, giving rise to distinct sociopolitical configurations and thus various collective identities and multiple scenarios of confrontation.

In conclusion, the combination of class and struggle, of action and subject in the Marxist narrative, configures a synthetic formula that allows for a dialectical escape from the structuralism-subjectivism duality without losing sight of the dynamic centrality of antagonism, of antagonist subjectivation as the trigger for the transformational processes set in motion by emancipatory impulses and desires. The notion of *antagonism* can therefore be conceived of as a fundamental theoretical element, a specifically Marxist one, that expresses the relationship between class and struggle, a relationship where struggle shapes class and class manifests itself as a political subjectivity by means of struggle.

Translated by Larry Goldsmith

References

Barker, C. (2013). Class Struggle and Social Movements. In C.Baker et al., *Marxism and Social Movements.* Brill.

Bensaid, D. (2003.) *Marx intempestivo. Grandezas y miserias de una aventura crítica*. Herramienta.

Bensaid, D. (2005). *La discordance des temps*. De la Passion.

Bensaid, D. (2010*). Marx for Our Times: Adventures and Misadventures of a Critique*. Verso.

Bidet, J.& Duménil, G. (2007). *Altermarxisme. Un autre marxisme pour un autre monde.* University of France

Bihr, A. (2012). *Les rapports sociaux de clases*. Page Deux.

Burawoy, M. & Wright, E.O. (2000). Sociological Marxism. In E.O. Wright, *Interrogating Inequality: Essays on Class Analysis, Socialism and Marxism*. Verso.

Corcuff, P. (2001). Marx et les nouvelles sociologies: les voies d'un dialogue dans l'après-décembre 1995. *Contretemps* 1.

Dardot, P. & Laval, C. (2012). *Marx, prénom: Karl.* Gallimard.

Gómez, M. (2014). *El regreso de las clases. Clase, acción colectiva y movimientos sociales.* Biblos.

Losurdo, D. (2013). *La lotta di classe. Una storia polìtica e filosòfica.* Laterza.

Marx, Karl. (1860). *Carta a Freiligrath.*

Mezzadra, S. (2014). *Nei cantieri marxiani. Il soggetto e la suaproduzione.* Manifestolibri.

Modonesi, M. (2014). *Subalternity, Antagonism, Autonomy: Constructing the Political Subject.* Pluto Press.

Modonesi, M. (2018). *The antagonistic principle. Marxism and political action.* Brill.

Therborn, G. (2014). *Del marxismo al posmarxismo?.* Akal.

Thompson, E. P. (1965). The Peculiarities of the English. *Socialist Register* 2.

Thompson, E. P. (1978). Eighteenth-Century English Society: Class Struggle without Class?. *Social History* 3.

Thompson, E. P. (1995). *The Poverty of Theory: Or an Orrery of Errors.* Merlin Press.

Van der Linden, M. (2013). Proletariado: conceito e polémicas. *Revista Outubro*, 21

Williams, R. (1977). *Marxism and Literature.* Oxford University Press.

Wood, E. M. (2000). La clase como proceso y como relación. In Wood, E.M. *Democracia contra capitalismo.* Siglo XXI.

Wood, E. M. (2013). *¿Una política sin clases? El post-marxismo y su legado.* RyR.

Wright, E.O. (1994). *Interrogating Inequality: Essays on Class Analysis, Socialism and Marxism.* Verso.

Wright, E. O. (2005). Social Class. In G. Ritzer (Ed.) *Encyclopedia of Social Theory.* Sage.

Notes on Contributors

Massimo Modonesi
Massimo Modonesi is a historian and sociologist, Professor at the Political and Social Sciences College in the Universidad Nacional Autónoma de México (UNAM). He is the author of 15 books and close to 200 articles on Marxist concepts and sociopolitical movements in Mexico and Latin America

Alfonso García Vela
Alfonso García Vela is professor and researcher in the Instituto de Ciencias Sociales y Humanidades, at the Benemérita Universidad Autónoma de Puebla, Mexico. His fields of research and teaching are sociology, Frankfurt School critical theory, modern social theory, and Western Marxism. His latest publication is *Open Marxism. Against a Closing World* (Pluto Press, 2020) co-edited with Ana Cecilia Dinerstein, John Holloway, and Edith González.

María Vignau Loría
María Vignau Loría is a Ph.D. Candidate in Sociology at the University of Washington. Her research agenda includes social theory, international migration, and demography.

Guido Liguori
Guido Liguori is a philosopher, professor at the Università della Calabria, in Italy. He is the president of the International Gramsci Society. His works include *Gramsci's Pathways* (Brill, 2015) and *Gramsci Contested: Interpretations, Debates and Polemics, 1922-2012* (Brill, 2022).

Matari Pierre Manigat
Matari Pierre Manigat is an economist, researcher at the Institute of Social Research in the Universidad Nacional Autónoma de México (UNAM). His work deals with the relationship between finance capital and the state.

ibidem.eu